# Emotional Intelligence

*21 Science of Awareness Techniques to Master Your Emotions, Improve Your Communication Skills, Enhance Your Leadership and Strengthen Relationships*

## Peter H. King

# Table of Contents

# Chapter One: An Introduction to Emotional Intelligence

## What is Emotional Intelligence?

Empathy is defined as the ability to feel sympathy and emotional towards another person. Emotional intelligence is when you have an awareness of your feelings and can monitor and control one's own emotional well-being, as well as recognize other people's emotions with a strong degree of sensitivity. Also known as EQ, emotional intelligence is comprised of several components or characteristics that define the presence and level of EQ:

## The Presence of Self-Awareness

To become self-aware emotionally is to understand your emotions and how they affect you and other people. Characteristics of self-awareness include maturity and self-confidence. Can you laugh at yourself and not take a joke too seriously? When someone else makes a joke in good faith, is it immediately upsetting or something you can take in stride? Being able to laugh at your mistakes is a good sign that you are confident and mature enough to achieve emotional self-awareness. On the other side, being aware of others' reactions and emotions shows you know how they perceive you are a good way to determine maturity.

## Regulation of Emotion

When you feel a strong emotion that evokes an equally strong response, it can be difficult to control for some people. The ability to use restraint and control impulsiveness in expressing one's emotions and gauging how to react to another person is important in regulation. For example, if a person begins shouting, we may know from experience that they tend to become easily frustrated and react quickly. In knowing this about a person, we may respond calmly, trying to diffuse the situation, instead of reacting in the same way. In a case where a person is unexpectedly angry, it can be due to an unusual circumstance or event that doesn't normally occur and showing a sympathetic and cautious attempt to communicate with them is the best way to show empathy and regulation of our emotions.

## Self-Improvement

Continuous self-improvement, an interest in developing and learning to better yourself and having the mindset to continue through difficult challenges are all signs of emotional strength and intelligence. This includes setting your own goals and having the drive to achieve them despite setbacks and obstacles. An example is when someone is motivated to improve their health and fitness by their own standards, or to obtain better education or understanding of other people. Self-improvement also means striving for goals that make you a better person internally, and not a way to become wealthy or obtain items to impress other people. If you fail at a course or fall short of achieving a goal, accepting the outcome, and trying again without giving up is a sign of emotional maturity and a strong will for improvement.

# Empathy

Empathy is the ability to understand other people's emotions and their reasons for acting in a certain way. One path to achieving empathy is learning to understand and accept our own feelings. For example, when we feel upset, we might react without thinking about the consequences or why we feel a certain way. Learning to take a moment to reflect on our emotions and taking time before we express them, can go a long way in how we impact others. Showing a genuine interest in other people's feelings and observing them with the intention of understanding them better shows empathy. Knowing when someone has endured a significant change or tragic circumstance, can help us react appropriately and with sensitivity. Anticipating certain reactions or expressions in specific situations can help us cope with other people and understand their different coping mechanisms. Sometimes, people behave differently in similar circumstances because of their own experiences and abilities to communicate. Where some people are open with expressing how they feel without hesitation, other people are subtler or less likely to show their inner thoughts and feelings. Becoming familiar with this difference is a good way to know other people better.

# Developing Social Skills

Good customer service skills, learning to communicate effectively and listen to others are all involved with developing good social skills. This also includes adapting to different types of humor, including sarcasm and jokes; knowing when to take someone seriously or not, and building strong interpersonal relationships and friendships. Taking ownership and leadership roles is a sign of emotional maturity, as well as time management and setting aside time to deal with other people in a compassionate and thoughtful manner. Developing social skills is not only an important part of improving emotional intelligence but also a way to succeed in how we connect with other people and identify with them.

## The History and Background of EQ (Emotional Intelligence)

The history of EQ or emotional intelligence originates from 1990, and the term was given to describe social intelligence and the ability to monitor emotions and reactions by Peter Salovey and John D. Mayer. Their research involved studying and monitoring how other people reacted emotionally to different films or situations that would normally evoke a wide variety of emotions and reactions. They also noted which participants in the studies were able to identify the type of emotion they were experiencing as well as how they perceived others and whether they were to accurately identify the emotional reaction in other people. In their findings, it was noticed that people who were more acutely aware of their own emotions as well as others, we're better equipped to handle social conflict and communicate effectively. This became the basis upon which a new class of intelligence and measuring its value was built for further study and understanding in society.

# Models of Emotional Intelligence: Understanding How EQ Works

In the early years of studying emotional intelligence, it has been debated whether some abilities are better honed and developed through cognitive abilities. While the study of cognitive function focused more on reasoning abilities, understanding more complex concepts and problem-solving, it did not provide an explanation on how to measure one's success in life. This is where emotional intelligence is beneficial in determining how we can thrive individually and within society on a more interpersonal, communicative, and behavioral level, as shown in the model below. Being aware of our own feelings, other's emotions and how we foster and develop relationships and communicate with other people are all part of building a strong EQ.

## Emotional Intelligence Model 1

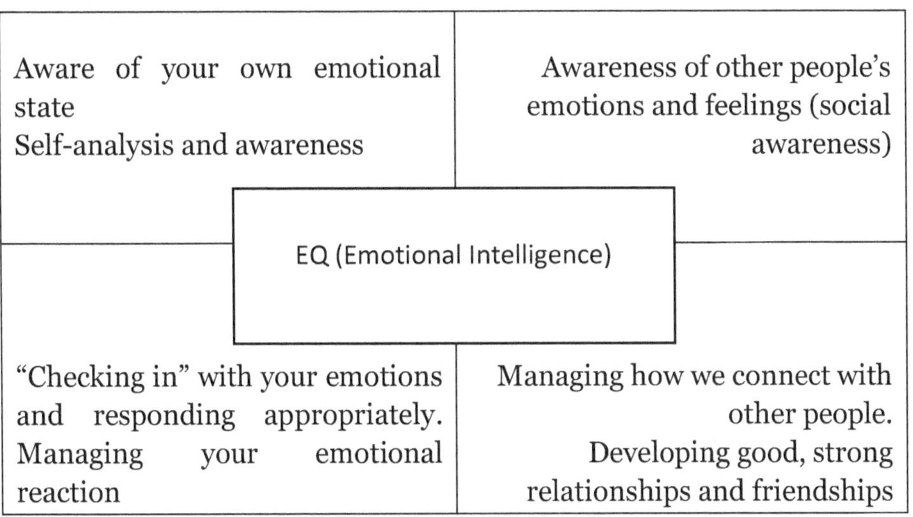

Another model of EQ or emotional intelligence is the improvement of self-control, which involves self-awareness and management of our reactions to other people and the way they interact with us. This process can be more challenging for some people than others, as it involves a significant degree of self-reflection and analysis. Self-control requires that we look within first, before reacting (thinking before we speak or act) and determining what is the best course of action, or if any action should be taken at all. The concept of developing self-control is to rid our emotions and reactions to others of as much negativity as possible. The following steps are part of the improvement and development of self-control within our daily lives:

**Emotional Intelligence Model 2: Self-Control Skills**

Recognizing the need for self-control as the first step in the process

Identify your emotional state: what are you feeling?

What is the cause or reason why you feel this way?

Think of how to respond positively and if not, defer a response until it necessary. Avoid

The way we feel can often be associated with specific experience, emotion, or circumstance. Sometimes we are readily aware of it, especially when a major event occurs, and we react accordingly. In other cases, we may not be aware of the source of our emotions, because they may be the result of experience or related association with something from our past that conjures certain feelings. Ascent, place, or object can, for some people, cause them to relive or re-experience a traumatic event or a joyous occasion, which results in an emotional reaction. Even when we choose to not express an emotion, it's important to know that we are experiencing a certain feeling. Achieving awareness is the first step to developing strong EQ skills.

The development of good listening skills is another trait of strong emotional intelligence. We often focus a lot on how we respond and communicate to others, with little or no attention to what they want to say. When we hear someone speaking to us, we may understand what they are saying, though may not comprehend much further than the content. When we actively listen, we do more than hear them; we seek to understand what they mean and the reasons for communicating with us. For example, when someone describes a nostalgic childhood vacation where they reminisce about a specific person or experience, we may attentively hear and understand what they are describing. When we listen to them and observe their non-verbal and verbal cues, we may notice subtle emotional reactions: they may feel contentment in their recollection of the experience, or a sense of sadness because they no longer experience the same feelings as they once did. If a person feels comfortable relating a specific personal experience or event, this may indicate a sense of trust or comfort. They may also feel that they are understood and worthy of listening too, which encourages them to communicate.

Good listening skills begin with patience. Often, people will appear to listen, with only the intention of waiting their turn to speak, and not truly understanding or absorbing what the other person is saying. When we pause to take time to actively engage in listening, without concern about when we can get a chance to speak, it means we are giving the other person a sense of understanding, and empathy, especially if they are disclosing something personal and meaningful. Becoming an active listener requires giving your undivided attention and making the other person aware of it so that they know that they are understood and listened to.

**Emotional Intelligence Model 3: Building Listening Skills**

| How to become an Active Listener: |
| --- |
| Step 1:<br>Show your focus: give your undivided attention and show your interest. Make eye contact, non-verbal gestures to acknowledge and actively engage with the speaker |
| Step 2:<br>Avoid interruption. Allow the speaker to finish completely before offering to contribute to the conversation. |
| Step 3:<br>If you are unsure whether the person speaking wants an opinion or feedback, ask them first. This can help avoid misunderstandings and possible conflicts. It also shows that you are paying attention and actively want to participate in a discussion or provide help. |
|  |

<table>
<tr><td>

<u>Step 4:</u>

When someone is finished speaking, acknowledge them. Let them know they were heard and if appropriate, express appreciation to them for sharing their experience. This can go a long way in validating what they have to say.

</td></tr>
<tr><td>

<u>Step 5:</u>

Give an honest and thoughtful response. If you disagree, be diplomatic and allow for a civilized conversation. If conflict results, simply explain that your response is honest and how you feel. This will allow the other person space for their own honest opinions and expressions.

</td></tr>
</table>

Following the above model and steps included will not always result in a perfect or ideal situation. In some scenarios, discussions, especially concerning controversial topics, can become heated and cause a lot of friction. When this occurs, step back and listen to the other side of the argument. Listening does not mean you agree with the other person; it is a way to understand them better and make sense of where they are coming from and why they have a specific opinion(s). Improving listening skills can also foster a stronger understanding of other people's ideas and ways of thinking in general.

Self-motivation refers to having your own "motor" or drive to achieve your own goals with little or no external motives. When you have the ambition to strive ahead, it is a powerful feeling, and you will stop at nothing to meet your goal. If your plan is to increase your ability to become self-motivated, focusing on your goal by visualizing success is a way to keep your progress on track. One of the most common occurrences with embarking on your own goals is feeling discouraged and wanting to give up when certain milestones aren't reached. Some people can become so focused on perfection and meeting every step of the way without error, that they feel disappointed when the results aren't as they expected. This is natural, though unrealistic, as most people will fail, often several times before they reach a point of success. Staying motivated for the long-term is key, and staying focused, as challenging as it may be, can be done with the right support and tools. The points below show how different attributes can boost your self-motivation and direct you on the right path to achieve your goals:

**Accepting Change:**

- As you work towards a goal, there will be unexpected changes and twists along the way. Accepting that changes will happen, and sometimes thwart your plans is vital to continue down the road to success. It won't always be easy, because some changes can effectively "derail" your plans, making it impossible to continue unless you start over again.

- A part of accepting change is understanding that the road to success isn't easy, especially if the task you wish to achieve is significant. Sometimes change can be simple, like a distraction that can delay our progress, though if the focus is maintained, the goal can be achieved.

**Taking Calculated Risks:**

- Working towards a goal is not smooth sailing. It often requires a lot of hard work and dedication. Understanding the gravity of the work involved sometimes means taking some risks, such as dedicating time, and sometimes money or resources to a project.

- Risk-taking must be done with caution and planning. A calculated risk stands a better chance of risk than a hasty decision, and should always have a plan B or C, just in case it doesn't unfold according to plan. Knowing when to take a risk and when it's not advantageous is crucial. If necessary, seek advice from someone with experience or knowledge that can provide feedback and ideas on how best to proceed.

**Positive Attitude:**

- Keeping a positive attitude is not easy and not always achievable, especially under a lot of stress and during long periods of hard work. Discouragement and setbacks are common contributors to losing positivity, which is natural. Maintaining a positive attitude doesn't necessarily mean ignoring or bypassing the negative aspects of the project, but merely acknowledging them and moving forward as best as possible

**High Emotional Intelligence:**

- A major part of the success of achieving a goal is improving emotional intelligence. Becoming aware of your emotions, responses and those of others involved in the project or goal. For example, working in a team environment can be challenging, though learning to work with people who may differ in opinion can be easier with a high EQ skill set.

## Delaying Short-term Gratification:

- The importance of delayed gratification will be discussed in chapter ____. It is important to delay the short-term, or more "immediate" results of gratification to focus on the long-term goals. Often, the immediate results are not only less significant, but they also make less of an impact on our overall success. While achieving milestones along the way is important, each step should contribute to the long-term goal, and not just as a source of gratification on its own.

- Focusing on the big goal at the end of the path is best for keeping focus. Short-term gratification can easily be a distraction and often an excuse to give up completely when other steps don't appear to be producing the results we want. Always focus on the long-term goal ahead.

## Enjoying a Challenge:

- People who are emotionally intelligent tend to embrace change and enjoy a challenge. This is beneficial in achieving self-motivation because it improves our sense of self and confidence overall. Some challenges are more exciting than others, while some can present more work and drawbacks than expected.

- Enjoying a challenge doesn't mean enjoying every step of the process, but the idea of conquering a difficult task or achieving a goal that may seem impossible. When we challenge ourselves, we are acknowledging that the road ahead is not going to be easy and that we might fail, and accept that despite those risks.

Emotional intelligence comes naturally for some people, while others can achieve a higher level of EQ will skill-building and applying techniques to develop their emotional and social awareness. The next section explains how applying EQ can change the outcome of a situation, and possibly improve it. In some cases, emotional and social awareness can simply give us a better understanding of what other people are going through, giving us an opportunity to adjust our way of responding to them.

## How Emotional Intelligence Applies in Everyday Life

Why is emotional intelligence measured and how is it important in everyday life? It impacts all aspects of our lives, including work, school, the relationships we have with our family and friends and how we experience the world around us. How we emote is essential to our life experience. For example, if a person is generally happy or feels content most of the time, they will likely get more out of life, than someone who is always finding the negative side and is easily frustrated. Sometimes there are good reasons for the way we express ourselves, and other times it can be impulsive and hasty.

When we decide solely based on our emotional response or feelings at a given time, we often do so in error. This is due to deciding quickly, and often without much thought beforehand. When we give ourselves time to contemplate a scenario or situation first, our choice on how to respond or act will differ significantly. Here are several examples of how acting impulsively, based on our immediate emotional response can affect the outcome of a situation:

**Example 1:**

During a train ride, one passenger becomes unruly and begins to talk loudly and offensively. This person walks down the aisles of the train, hurling insults at random. They might approach you and make a gesture or comment, which is hurtful and causes a sensation of anger or frustration. In that instant, making a quick decision on how to react could mean shouting back in response with a strong statement, which may escalate the situation to a dangerous event, with possible violence. By the time someone can intervene, the damage may already be done. It may impact other people around you, including passengers and staff.

In approaching the situation from a more proactive angle, the best action to take is observation. Look for personnel or alert someone to safety, as the situation has dangerous potential. There may be unknown factors for the person's actions, which may play a role in their behavior, but more importantly, remaining safe and noticing other people's reactions is equally, if not more vital. Always search for a peaceful means to diffuse or resolve a situation that could be potentially harmful. If a person insults or threatens you directly, responding in a calm manner may be of more use and could minimize the situation. Once the situation is settled, further action can be taken to deal with the offending person.

**Example 2:**

A co-worker shows up late on a regular basis and always has a story or excuse. At first, no one minds, though once they begin to show up late to staff meetings and leave early without giving notice, it becomes a nuisance. The office gossip spreads about the co-worker, accusing them of laziness or being irresponsible, and although they tend to finish their projects at work and perform well, they gradually miss more deadlines as time passes, prompting a meeting with human resources to address their performance issues.

In a meeting with the personnel manager, they are reprimanded for their tardiness and not achieving their deadlines on time. The co-worker becomes emotional to the point of crying and apologizing for the decline in their work ethic. The personnel manager provides them with a plan of action as a means to improve their performance, or face disciplinary action, though they do not give the employee an opportunity to provide an explanation for their change in work habits, nor do they appear to acknowledge the stress caused by this meeting. The employee has been with the company for close to ten years and has only recently started changing their performance level at work.

An emotionally intelligent method of handling this situation would be to approach the employee with compassion, and consider some key points in their work history with the company:

- For the past ten years, the employee has had a stellar record of work performance, which has only changed in the past couple of months
- There may be factors beyond the scope of the workplace that may trigger the employee to behave differently, such as a tragic event, or occurrence that is impacting their schedule
- Asking the employee if there is anything they would like to discuss, in a calm, private and confidential matter, without

bringing any attention or spreading rumors around the office is an important step in establishing trust, and a means to communicate more effectively

- The possibilities of what may be causing an employee to suddenly change their work habits can vary extensively, from grieving the death of a close family member or friend, suffering from depression or a condition that affects their sense of well-being, to having to escape from domestic violence. There are many other examples, though these are common possibilities and should be addressed delicately and compassionately before further action is taken.

Providing emotional support is as simple as listening intently and making sure the other person knows you are interested in what they have to say. Some people face difficult challenges on their own with little or no support and giving them an "ear" can be a major source of comfort and help put them at ease.

**Example 3:**

A friend or relative's child is grieving the loss of their pet dog. Their death occurred suddenly when the dog became scared and ran into the street and was instantly struck by an oncoming truck. Although the child didn't see the incident, they are traumatized and inconsolable. When they approach their parents, they are told that they should not cry but look forward to adopting a new puppy soon. With the best of intentions, the child's parents feel that by adopting a new pet, the grieving will fade, and everyone will be able to carry on as usual. This isn't the case, because the dog was a part of the family's household since the birth of their child for nearly ten years.

Some people view a pet as a family member, while others may not feel this way. In any case, losing someone very close is an emotionally painful experience that doesn't simply disappear after a specific amount of time. When the parents offer to adopt a new pet as a "replacement", it doesn't help console their child, because the grieving process takes time. The parents are grieving as well, though they fail to recognize or acknowledge their true feelings, and instead, look for a way to resolve the "gap" of not having a pet as a coping mechanism. What they don't realize, is that by not acknowledging how they really feel, they are delaying the grieving process, and it may affect them later. Adopting a new pet may help them cope, though the sadness of losing a cherished pet will remain for some time.

The process of grieving is complex. There are at least five stages to grieving, and they vary for everyone. Some people may progress through each stage quickly, while others may endure years of each phase. A loss will stay will us for a very long time, sometimes for the rest of our life. It's important to understand that each stage of grief is valid and healthy to experience:

1. The first stage is denial, and for many, it's experienced as a feeling of numbness or a state of shock. It's our mind's way of protecting us from the impact of the loss, which may be severe. It's a necessary step because it helps us to continue initially on "autopilot", going to work, continuing regular tasks and routines without interruption. Denial keeps us in survival mode so that we don't have time to think too much about the event, which has just occurred.

2.  Anger is the next stage. We may feel that what happened was unfair or unjust. Some people question their beliefs and wonder why such a loss occurred. Anger is the result of feeling that the pain from the event is undeserved, not only for the one who is gone but for those who are left to suffer the loss. In society, anger is an emotion that we are used to managing, knowing that it can easily escalate and become uncontrollable. When this happens, people will see a side to a person that they never imagined existed, because what they are going through his inconceivable. Along with the anger, are feelings of abandonment, even if there is no intention of doing so.

3.  The next stage is often known as the bargaining phase, where someone will actively think of what they could have done to prevent the occurrence, even if there was nothing that could have been foreseen. They may also consider making significant changes to avoid feeling the same pain again, including a serious lifestyle change or showing more affection to the ones they love. It may stem from a sense of guilt, as many people will blame themselves, even if there is no fault. The phase of guilt and bargaining can last a while, and return at a later stage in life when other stages of the grieving process are experienced.

4.  Depression is one of the most difficult phases of the grieving process. The full brunt or heaviness of the loss is felt during this stage and can cause a person to become non-functional in many ways, from being unable to care for themselves and communicate with others about their loss. Many people will retreat and avoid contact because they feel misunderstood or

judged. Often, people are expected to "get over it" within a year or two, though there is no definitive timeline for grief. As painful and heartbreaking as this stage is, it is completely necessary and natural to experience and endure for as long as it takes. Having a good support system and acknowledging your feelings can help you feel validated and understood, especially if there are others going through the same process.

5. The final stage, which may come sooner or much later, is acceptance. The stage of acceptance doesn't mean there is no more sadness or depression. There could remain traces of anger and denial at times though overall, you will eventually come to a state of accepting that what happened cannot be changed or reversed and focus on moving forward as best possible. Some people become busy with many activities or continue with the bargaining process, to "make amends" for what they consider to be their fault.

After all stages of the grieving process are experienced, they may be revisited at some point, or some stages may come before others. Grief is different for everyone, and not everyone copes in the same way. Some people will experience all five stages in sequence, while others may skip or repeat one or more phases. There are those of us who will go to work, continue, as usual, wearing the mask of denial, while we gradually progress through each stage until we reach acceptance. Other people will make a complete overhaul of their lives when grieving sets in. It varies extraordinarily for everyone.

The most important role in each of the three examples is to recognize and acknowledge your feelings at the moment while making the effort to do the same for others. If we stop initially to simply absorb those feelings, we give ourselves a chance to understand what those emotions are, and why. This allows us to make a more informed decision regarding how we react and gives us a chance to make a more reasonable, well-thought-out response, as opposed to a quick reaction that can lead to conflict and misunderstanding.

# Chapter Two: Understanding and Improving Emotional Intelligence

This section covers the methods we can use to improve our overall understanding of each other and improve our emotional intelligence. This includes becoming self-aware of how we act and behave in specific situations, to ensure that we are responding sensitively or appropriately where necessary. Not every scenario calls for the same style of comment or feedback, even if we simply see it as our way of communicating. Developing social and emotional maturity means adapting and switching our mode of communication to show that we understand or want to relate and empathize. It can also be a way to make ourselves heard in a more impactful way, rather than simply reacting in a fit of anger or outburst.

## What is Self-awareness and How Does this Apply to Emotional Intelligence

Self-awareness is having a clear perception of our personality, how our actions and behaviors affect others. It means reflecting carefully on past events to determine if we reacted appropriately in certain situations, and how we can improve on them in the future. This practice is ongoing and shows a deep level of emotional intelligence. Self-awareness begins with our own self-monitoring and becoming mindful and aware of how we communicate, react, and express ourselves to other people, including those we connect with on a regular basis, such as family and co-workers. Sometimes we may react in a way that seems impulsive to someone else, but normal or familiar to us.

What does it mean to be fully aware of ourselves? When we know how we are feeling and why we also understand where this experience will take us. As an example, picture yourself in a job that you worked hard to obtain. It was a goal you set your eyes on five years ago, and with enough perseverance, taking extra courses and proving your skills and abilities to your employer, you were promoted to a senior management position. Sometimes, when we achieve what we want, the perspective changes. The "high" of achieving the goal is a positive experience, and the promotion has perks that include a good salary and better working conditions, though it may also not be exactly what we envisioned. It's completely acceptable to be disappointed in a goal, though many people who feel this way, simply brush off the idea, and convince themselves that they should simply accept their fate, as it was what they worked so hard for, and to make a change would be considered "giving up". For many people, the reality is continuing in a career they are less than thrilled with because it is a steady source of income and employment for the foreseeable future. What happens when we see our true feelings about the promotion and acknowledge them? It can either prompt us to continue anyway and finding another means of escaping our situation through hobbies or interests. This realization may also encourage a person to switch careers altogether or take a completely different path in life. Either way, being aware of our selves means we are living our true lives. We can continue however we choose, though we are now aware of our options and our decisions for and against them.

The quick method of conducting a self-analysis is to initially be aware of thought when you have one and determine how your emotional reaction at that moment. Identifying the thought and that it's occurring it the first step. The second step is identifying your emotion, as it occurs with the thought. The third and final step in this quick process is to actively respond to the thoughts and emotions you are having at the moment and taking steps to resolve or react responsibly to them. For example, if an image of someone getting more acceptance or praise for a project that you equally participated in, the first thought you may have been "Why them? Why do they get all the credit for a lot of the effort I put into this?" At that moment, the emotion you may be experiencing could be jealousy, anger, or both. This covers the first two steps in the quick analysis. In determining how we react, we might take a moment to become calm before we address our lack of praise, or, simply say nothing at all and accept that the incident was unfair, and nothing further can be said or done to remedy it.

The process of self-analysis, whether it is a quick "check-in", as the above example, or a deeper assessment of our feelings and actions, it is an exercise that effectively promotes and increases emotional maturity, which improves emotional intelligence. Taking the time and effort to realize the importance of this self-analysis exercise is already a step towards improving EQ.

# How to Identify Areas of Development and Improvement

There is always room for growth and improvement when it comes to emotional intelligence, and this includes people who may have achieved a strong awareness of their EQ already. For everyone, there is always room for improvement and areas to identify for improvement:

## Being Assertive

Assertiveness is often mistaken for aggressive behavior, though there is a significant difference. Aggressive communication can be intimidating and may come across as threatening in some cases. It is often a reactionary response, and not thought out in advance. People who shout or lash out at others with no consideration beforehand risk being aggressive. Assertiveness, on the other hand, is direct, firm and gives you the opportunity to command respect, without showing aggression or negative emotion, such as anger or fear. Being assertive is simply about being direct with other people when you communicate with them. If someone asks you a question that may be difficult to answer, some people avoid a direct response out of fear or become passive and intimidated. If they behave aggressively, it may indicate that they are attempting to hide something. Assertiveness is the best option as it simply states the answer to the question, even if it is not favorably received. In being direct, you also show honesty and transparency, which go a long way to establishing trust and better communication in the future.

## Don't React; Learn to Respond

Being reactive simply means we simply reply or react without any prior thinking or reflection on the situation we are responding to. When this happens, we often say something regrettable and hurtful. This can result in misunderstandings and people may avoid connecting or communicating with someone who is always reacting without thinking before they speak. Responding is different from reacting, as it takes at least a little bit of thought before something is said or done. Effectively responding to a challenging or triggering comment can be as simple as taking a few seconds to formulate a thoughtful response. In a short period of time, we have an opportunity to find something less abrasive or upsetting, as that quick few seconds gives us time to absorb first, respond after, while reacting is immediate.

## Show Empathy

Unfortunately, a lot of people see the showing of emotion as a sign of weakness, not strength. They may consider that a person crying in public is brave or simply grieving beyond their ability to control their emotional reactions. This unrealistic view of emotional expression has contributed significantly to how many societies and individuals suppress their feelings and continue to smile, even when they are crying inside. Showing empathy to others doesn't necessarily imply the full expression of sadness, anger, or fear, but to acknowledge it and let the other person know that what they are relating to you is having an impact. Non-verbal cues, such as nodding, maintaining eye contact, and moving closer to provide an embrace or another acceptable reassurance with a pat on the back or shoulder, can go a long way to providing comfort and indicating that you want to be supportive and understanding.

## Become Approachable

Socializing doesn't come naturally to everyone. Some people prefer their solitude over social groups and events. For other people, socializing is effortless, and they can often read gestures and cues to determine how they will communicate with someone before they do. People who possess good social skills are often well-liked and easy to approach and talk to. The more quiet, reserved type of person is often viewed as shy or unapproachable simply because they do not talk much or engage often with other people. Their personality is virtually unknown, which can seem risky because we may not know how they will react. If we are the quiet type of person, it's completely natural, though it can hinder our progress where communication is a good trait. Becoming approachable doesn't mean we have to suddenly talk with everyone and converse at every opportunity, though making eye contact and a friendly greeting or comment can make a significantly different from awkward and unknown to friendly and approachable. If making small talk isn't your type of communication, smiling and nodding is a good way to greet someone without talking about the weather or the weekend. Once you create a positive rapport with people, they will be more apt to take the initiative and approach you first, which may be more comfortable for some people. Socializing may become more natural over time, once you gradually get more familiar with others.

## Accept Constructive Criticism

Not all criticism is negative and can often be constructive. We may not always see the constructive side to constructive criticism. It can cause people to take offense and react harshly. The next section discusses the benefits of constructive criticism and how it can become some of the best advice we need. Sometimes the advice we think we need isn't what we want to hear. When the message is delivered, we tend to recoil and react with disdain and anger. A lot of the criticism we receive, whether constructive or not, can serve some form of purpose based on its source and the reason(s) for why it was expressed.

## Using Feedback and Constructive Criticism to your Benefit

Criticism, even when it is meant to be constructive and helpful, can seem like an attack on our abilities and intentions. A lot of people will react to constructive criticism in a negative way, taking it personally, even when it comes from a valid source or person who has their best interest at heart. Sometimes, it is difficult to accept, when our perception of a situation is vastly different than others see it. Constructive criticism may be hard to swallow, though it can provide a window of opportunity for self-improvement. Here are some helpful tips on how to use constructive criticism to your benefit:

- Focus on the situation that is central to the critique, and not the person or people who are making the statement or criticism. For example, if we write a report on a specific topic that we are familiar with, it is upsetting to receive criticism on how the piece was written or how we chose to present it. If the criticism, however constructive, originates from someone who tends to be difficult to please or often makes critical comments, it can be hard to avert attention from the person, though this is the first step to shifting focus back to the core issue, which is the report.

- If constructive criticism seems more accusatory in nature, ask what suggestions or recommendations are available for improvement. This essentially changes a negative comment into a positive action, which can become proactive in the future. If a person truly wants to be constructive in their critique, they will be able to give some recommendations and show a willingness to help.

- If you feel hurt or impacted by the harshness of constructive criticism, which can come across as abrasive from some people, speak in terms of how you feel, to let them know the effect it has on you. For example, if someone makes a statement that focuses on what you need to improve, and that your efforts are not good enough, ask them what the expectation is. Sometimes, we are not provided with the full scope of expectations for a given project or task. When this happens, the results of our work can fall short in achieving a goal. Always let the person know where you stand, what your understanding of the situation is and how you feel at the moment. This will give them an opportunity to adjust their response to a more well-thought-out one.

When criticism is not constructive, it can be difficult to overlook or ignore, especially if it feels personal. While some people criticize with the intention of giving you some direction towards improvement, they may not always know how to express their thoughts diplomatically and come across negatively. It's always best to respond with probing questions, such as:

- I understand that you are not satisfied with my work. May I ask what I can do to meet your expectations?
- I feel personally attacked by what you said. I also want to understand why you made that statement/remark. Can you explain what you mean by (state item/issue)?
- I appreciate your feedback and want to make improvements. Can you provide advice or recommendations for me?

Sometimes, criticism is unkind, unwarranted, and not constructive at all. When people make purposeful insults or upsetting comments, it can be easy to react and feel hurt. At that moment, it's best to consider the source of the comments and/or statements and avoid responding at all. In cases where a person is persistent in criticizing you, without any reason, you can attempt to ask them why, though be prepared for an irrational and sometimes stronger (or meaner) response.

## Self-analysis and "Checking in" with your Emotions and Emotional Responses

Practicing self-analysis is crucial to establishing a good sense of EQ and taking time to understand others. Unless we understand how we behave emotionally and why we'll never begin to comprehend the way other people react and communicate. Self-analysis or self-assessment gives us a chance to better understand where we can build more confidence, understand how we view ourselves and how we incorporate the feelings of others into our own self-image or sense of self.

## What Exactly is Self-Analysis?

It's not a test, and there are no right or wrong answers. It is more reflective of how well you know yourself and helps you gain a better understanding of you. This includes the type of personality you have, what your goals are, your interests, ideals, and values. Over time, these may change, as we grow older and adapt to different environments and situations. For example, starting a new career may feel more exciting and spark a sense of ambition, whereas remaining in a job or career that doesn't pan out the way we envision, could result in feelings of boredom or stagnancy. Our priorities and values may change depending on what path we take in life, such as starting a family, or embarking on a life-long career or moving to another country. When this occurs, our self-analysis may look completely different. Sometimes a change in self-confidence or significant experience can impact our emotional intelligence and how we see or understand ourselves.

## Why is a Self-Assessment a Good Idea?

When someone asks you to tell them about yourself, how do you answer? Do you state your line of work or expertise, whether you are a full-time college student, a parent or the hobbies and interests you have? These are all part of us, though they are surface attributes and do not give a real in-depth, full version of us. For example, we may have a passion for helping stray animals and volunteering at a local shelter to support your greater community. This gives people more about the kind of person we are because of what we do or enjoy getting involved in. We may also describe who we are more than what we do, such as stating that you are sensitive, strive to be fair and just, or on the other side, you may admit your faults, which could be impatience or impulsiveness. In giving more of "you" than "what you do", you effectively provide a glimpse into your level of emotional intelligence. For a person to acknowledge certain faults, passions and/or sensitivities, they are communicating on a deeper, more personal level that can resonate with others and improve communication. Self-analysis gives us a better way to look deeper within and understand more about who we are.

## How to Conduct a Self-analysis or Self-assessment

To be as accurate and effective as possible, a self-assessment should refer to different aspects of a person's life to extract the values in each of them, as follows:

**Values related to work or career:**

- Do you enjoy working individually or within a team, or both? Some people find they prefer having control over certain decisions within a department or organization, while other people are more comfortable taking orders

- Can you cope with an unstable or constantly changing environment? Does the idea of thriving in chaos excite you, or do you prefer a more stable, predictable place to work? For some people, chaos is their life and they thrive on the stress and jumping from one project to another. Working as a medical professional in the emergency department of a hospital or as a stunt performer are vastly different careers, though they provide constant change and can be unpredictable, as there is risk involved. Some people are always switching jobs, never satisfied with where they work, where other people remain with a company for the long term.

- Is money the most important driver in which career or job you choose or are there other factors, such as convenience, stability, and other benefits such as job satisfaction or a passion for a certain line of work or business?

**Hobbies and interests:**

- What do you enjoy doing in your spare time when you don't have to work or tend to other commitments?  The hobbies and interests we choose can often predict the type of work we do, and the type of people we enjoy associating with, including co-workers.  Some people are more apt to be physically active and enjoy sports, marathons, and exercise that challenges their abilities and helps them improve health and agility.  In their career, they may employ similar techniques, challenging themselves with a new project that may be riskier than usual, or asking for a promotion.  People who are more interested in reading, writing, arts, and crafts, maybe more creative, though also may seek work where they can apply their abilities in a constructive way.  Our choice of interests also indicates how we approach situations involving our feelings and the emotions of others.  If we are more analytical and enjoy writing reports or research, we may appear subtler in our emotions and more straight-forward in relating information. People who are more artistic, creative, or ambitious are prone to more emotional expression, and usually not afraid to show how they feel openly.

**Natural Talents:**

- When we consider skill sets and how we apply what we learn and apply the education we acquire, we may not realize our own natural abilities

- Are you naturally a quick learner, easy to adapt to challenging and changing situations, or and can you balance multiple demands or tasks at once? Some people are more people-focused and in-tune with their EQ, while others are more task-oriented and focus on the goal in such a way that they are not easily distracted or discouraged.

- Other talents may include good writing skills, coming up with creative solutions or "thinking outside the box" or strong mathematical aptitude

The above examples of self-analysis can be helpful for anyone, especially for career planning and determining which path is best for your future. There are other ways to self-analyze to determine where you stand in terms of your self-esteem and how well you improve your ability to connect with your emotions and others' feelings.

**Developing Confidence:**

This is not the easiest task for many people, as to how we perceive ourselves is directly linked to the way we think other people see us. When we gaze through online forums and social media, it doesn't take long to feel as though other people are enjoying life more than us, and this is the biggest flaw with online profiles: they are almost always inaccurate, as people will paint the picture of their life as they want to appear to others, not as they actually feel. We may measure our progress in life with other people, and think we are doing much worse than them, even if that's not true. Body image, career success, and relationship goals are constantly evolving online and distorting our reality when we continue to compare ourselves with other people. There are more realistic and solid ways to improve your self-confidence that does not involve comparison:

- Compete against yourself instead of others. Make self-improvement for the sake of getting better at something or improving your own sense of self for the sake of just that. If we get distracted by how well we think someone else is doing in life, it doesn't help our own cause.

- Consider that other people are looking to you in the same way that you view them. We may project an image of what we want other people to see when they think of us. They may, similarly, inflate or distort their sense of self in comparison to us. The image is a slippery slope and can affect everyone. Celebrities are a good example of how people perceive them differently (as the people they have portrayed us, rather than regular people).

- Building confidence often means trying new things and managing what life throws at us, especially when it is unexpected. We are often stronger and more resilient than we think, and unless we take a risk now and again to prove that we are capable, we won't know. In achieving new talents and learning how to navigate through new challenges, confidence will grow.

Confidence is knowing when to take pride in your achievements and abilities, while remaining compassionate and kind, with no arrogance or negative attitude towards others. People are drawn to confidence, as they see it as something they want in their lives. What they often don't realize is that it's achieved from within, and not given by someone else's approval or acceptance of who we are.

**Communicate Honestly with Yourself and Others**

Do you often communicate how you feel or how certain events or situations, even people impact you? It's important to communicate to ourselves though letting other people know about our true feelings and thoughts is a sign of emotional maturity.

- When we talk to ourselves, are we critical? Do we doubt or question everything we do, or accept mistakes and rationalize them? How we communicate within makes a big difference in how we see ourselves and communicate with others. Most importantly, recognizing how we feel during those inner conversations is vital to understanding why we may have a certain thought process or trend. For example, we may blame everything on someone else, and use our inner conversation to rationalize our mistakes, even if we are at fault (even partially).
- Talking through difficult experiences and challenging thought processes can help us sort through what is going on in our minds. It's a good coping mechanism, if we remain constructive and, in some cases, even critically constructive. For every error we find with ourselves, it's best to talk through different methods and ideas for future improvement. Talking through certain steps of a procedure can help you absorb the information better, by internalizing it. This will also give you good practice on how to communicate and help other people

## Acting

After all the thinking, self-reflection and communicating within is done, it's time to act. Planning for the future career or making plans to build friendships or network with other people in business will only materialize if you simply make the effort. Many people will make plans with the best intentions, though stop short of completing the task. This is due to fear of failure or how they are perceived by others. In using the above tools to build confidence, moving to the "doing" phase of planning, by acting becomes more real and achievable.

## "Checking in" with our Emotions and the Emotions of Others

In a typical day, we may get so caught up in work, family, and social commitments, that we forget to check how we feel. In not checking in with our own feelings, we often skip doing this process with others as well. After a long day of work, asking your spouse and/or family how their day was is usually a conversation starter, that leads to discussing certain routine occurrences, people, and events. It rarely becomes a topic that discusses how the day made a person feel. A way of checking in can be as simple as changing the direction of the conversation as follows:

- How was it today for you? If you must assign an emotion to your day, in general, what would it be?
- How would you rate your day, on a level of one to ten, where one is calm, uneventful, and ten is highly stressful?

If someone expresses that they had a good day:

- Is there anything specific that "made" your day?

- What were the highlights of your day?  What would make it even better?

If a negative reaction occurs, probe further to find out if they are interested in discussing it more:

- Is there anything you want to talk about?  I'm here to listen
- If there was one thing you could change about your day to make it much better, what would it be?

Sometimes people are hesitant to discuss certain matters, especially if they are personal and sensitive.  Applying emotional intelligence in this case and when communicating with other people, it's important to let them know that you are open and willing to listen without judgment or, if needed, without feedback.  Listening on its own can be very effective invalidating someone else's feelings and experiences.

## How to Recognize Emotions based on Physiological Reactions

Physiological reactions occur when we react physically to an event or situation that causes an immediate gesture or movement.  It's often done without any thought, like a reflex.  When a person experiences fear, they may panic, experience shaky hands and sweaty palms.  This may also occur when a person becomes nervous or worried about public speaking, as an example.  Phobias are extreme fears that can cause a significant amount of physiological reactions in people, from visibly shaking to distorted speech and the appearance of panic.  The person experiencing these symptoms may also notice heart palpitations and short breaths, which may or may not be visible.  All these signs indicate fear or nervousness, and sometimes anxiety.

It's important to note that not all symptoms of anxiety, fear or nervousness are the same in every person. Some people's physiological reactions are very pronounced and obvious, while other people, who may experience fear and nervousness often, may show slight signs if any at all. Since many physiological symptoms are experienced internally, such as a faster heartbeat or shortness of breath, we may detect them in our selves before we recognize them in someone else. When someone becomes angry, they may appear to be calm on the exterior, though internally, their body becomes tense and they may grind their teeth or purse their lips as a more external gesture.

## Responding to Physiological Reactions

When you notice someone exhibiting a physiological reaction, how can you respond? The first key is to notice their reaction and reflect on what it means. If a person becomes withdrawn or tense in their posture or poses during a controversial topic of discussion, they may be showing discontent towards a specific point of view or statement. They may also be displeased by the topic in general, and choose to internalize their frustration, instead of vocalizing it. In recognizing a physiological reaction as a sign of displeasure or discontentment, approaching the person or situation directly, and calmly, is often the best method:

"You seem uncomfortable with this discussion. Would you like to change the topic?"

This statement does two things: it acknowledges that the other person appears to be uncomfortable, which indicates that we are paying attention and showing a degree of emotional maturity. Secondly, it provides a way to remedy the situation, should the other person feel uncomfortable, by offering to change the direction of the conversation. This can help diffuse a tense situation and possibly prevent an escalation of the conflict.

In a case where a person exhibits signs of fear, by visibly shaking or panicking, it can be difficult to speak to them directly, as they are preoccupied with an object or situation that is causing them to feel this way. They may actively look to leave the area and choose to not communicate at all. In the event, they remain, either because they cannot leave or choose not to, there are some things we can say to bring comfort and provide support:

"If you are nervous, it's ok, this is a stressful situation. If you want to talk about it, I'm here to listen."

These statements aim to achieve a few goals: to offer comfort to the other person by identifying what they may be feeling (nervousness or fear), acknowledging that their feelings are valid (it's a stressful situation) and offering to listen if they are comfortable discussing it. Simply hearing these words can give someone comfort, even if they choose not to engage. They will realize that you are ready to connect with them on an emotional level, even if just to provide momentary comfort and a distraction from their feelings.

There are also signs of joy, contentment, and excitement, all of which are generally considered positive emotions. Physiological reactions to these emotions include smiling, laughing, jumping, clapping, or giving a "high five" or other social gestures to show happiness. It's always a good idea to notice people experiencing something positive and giving them a congratulatory comment or nod. This helps reinforce your support of them, especially if it's to celebrate a milestone or major achievement with friends or family. Usually, a simple "congratulations" or "way to go! Well done!" is satisfactory for someone we may not know well, as we may say more words of encouragement to a close family member or friend.

Sometimes, physiological reactions are best observed without a reaction, as some people may not take well to interaction, especially if they try to minimize their reactions in public. In some cases, we may see more of one person's emotional side than they want us to see. Taking a cautious approach, and in some cases, assuring the other person that you may understand and empathize with them, in private, is the safest way to communicate. They may, in some cases, explain more to you later about a specific person or situation that cannot be easily stated in public.

# Chapter Three: The Power of Delayed Gratification

## Delayed Gratification: What is it and How Does it work?

Most people thrive on immediate gratification, and the more they achieve it, the more they strive for. It can be a great motivator in many ways, though we can lose sight of long-term goals when the gratification becomes more challenging or further from our immediate reach. Knowing when to strive towards a goal, despite there being no immediate or short-term rewards can be daunting and discouraging to most of us. It means taking longer and putting more effort into a goal that can take a significant amount of time to achieve, and when we are already saturated in a pattern of getting what we want quickly, reaching further be pointless. There are some good reasons why reaching for long-term goals and delayed gratification works:

- Long-term goals are usually more rewarding, and especially when they are successful after a long time period. In the end, they feel a more gratifying and short-term burst of gratification pale in comparison.

- Once you become adjusted to focusing solely on the long-term goal, you gain a better sense of self-control in your life and actions.

- The short-term gratification is short-lived and almost never beneficial for the long-term, even if it is tempting. Cheating on a healthy diet may satisfy a strong craving, though it

produces no actual benefit and can thwart further success
with the goal of losing weight or eating healthier as a habit.

- Visualize the benefits of achieving the long-term, or "big" goal
  in a way that stops you from becoming distracted from the
  smaller forms of gratification...

- Define short-term gratification as simply a distraction from
  the major goals, which will make a much better impact on
  your life and the quality of it. When we begin to see short-
  term goals for their reality, we sharpen our boundaries and
  strengthen the focus for the major achievements.

## Employing Methods of Delayed Gratification

There are several methods to apply delayed gratification. When
considering how to initially approach a project or goal, fix your
attention and drive towards a finishing line or the ultimate
achievement. Creating a strategy can be invaluable in improving all
aspects of life, including:

- Building a long-term career by focusing on big goals and
  ignoring the distractions along the way

- Improving how you handle and budget finances. Delayed
  gratification requires forgoing small, immediately gratifying
  rewards and focusing solely on more important expenses, so
  that money isn't wasted.

- Betterment of our health, mental and physical well-being.
  Focusing on a new diet or healthier way of eating means
  aiming towards a more sustainable, long-term goal and

avoiding pitfalls along the way that may give you a brief sense of satisfaction only

- Developing relationships and friendships. Seeing people as more than just their exterior and getting to know them authentically. Communicating and becoming emotionally aware of how they feel in specific situations, will help people bond and understand each other more fully

What is an example of delayed gratification? How is it useful in your life? The following examples provide realistic scenarios that show how the benefits of delayed gratification can make a significant improvement in how you accomplish tasks and achieve goals.

**Scenario 1:**

Karen is determined to lose about fifty pounds before the summer begins. It's late February, and she has always struggled with her weight, despite eating healthy and keeping moderately active. A recent doctor's visit indicated that Karen is in relatively good health, though she suffers from several allergies and high blood pressure. She was also diagnosed with high blood sugar, which means despite all the healthy eating, her diet remains full of sugar and with a significant level of carbohydrates. This news is a bit unexpected, though Karen is grateful there is nothing seriously wrong. She is offered the choice of taking medication to lower her blood pressure or adjust her diet to eliminate sugars and reduce carbohydrates. While this seems like a great idea, Karen finds the prospect of avoiding sugar perplexing. She is, however, determined to stick with a new diet and plans to lose the weight. To get started, she purchases several books on the ketogenic diet and how to prevent diabetes with low carb eating. As of the first week of March, she is ready to go.

The long-term goal is to follow the new way of eating, with the key to lose the fifty pounds by July. This gives Karen four full months of eating well and reducing the blood sugar, cholesterol, and blood pressure levels. By July, she will be ready for the beach! The prospect sounds great, and determination impacts Karen to the point where she shares her journey with co-workers and neighbors. Some of them take an interest in her goal, while others are indifferent. For support, Karen makes a couple of new friends at the local gym and asks them about the way they eat and how they achieved their ideal weight. She finds the social aspect of exercise as an added benefit and begins to lose significant weight within the first month. By mid-April, she is down twenty pounds and it is visible at work. Many co-workers take notice and Karen is complimented on her commitment and success. A couple of her friends, who are also co-workers, decide to follow the same diet plan. The three co-workers, plus the two new friends from the gym form a strong support network for Karen.

One day, Karen meets Henry, who works as a manager for a local restaurant. He's also a chef and makes some of the most delicious salads and seafood dishes Karen has ever tried. She is intrigued by him, and they begin to date. Henry met Karen after she had successfully lost thirty-five pounds, making the goal weight only fifteen more pounds to lose. When she explains her goal, Henry respects her hard work and dedication, though maintains a different point of view: he explains that the aim, while admirable, is not the best idea, because eliminating too much sugar is not natural. He suggests that doctors are only looking out for their own benefits, to make money off prescriptions and to "push" new diets that are not sustainable. Then, Henry treats Karen to a homemade dessert of custard and freshly baked apples with cinnamon. She hesitates at first, realizing that this isn't the best choice for her diet, but he convinces her to give it a try. It's only an occasional treat, and since she has been successful in losing weight and maintaining health goals, the dessert is a celebration of her achievement so far.

Over the next month, Henry entices Karen with more of his culinary creations, and she bends to his will, not wanting to offend him and instead, show appreciation for his talent. After a while, she considers asking Henry to make less sugary foods, and try something low carb, though every time he offers her yet another treat, she simply accepts it. Henry has convinced her to live life to the fullest, enjoy good food and not worry about what the doctor says. Karen is convinced for a while until she begins to gain some of the weight back that she had lost. When this happens, Henry reassures her that she looks wonderful, though Karen feels anxious and unhappy with the relapse. She fades further back into eating more high carb foods and by July, she's nearly back where she began. This creates tension in the relationship, and Karen feels as though nothing was achieved.

**Analysis of Scenario 1:**

Initially, Karen focused on the long-term goal of weight loss and improving her overall health, which could be easily achieved by following several dietary changes over a period of several months. In maintaining consistency towards the long-term goal of four months, Karen makes some significant strides ahead, until Henry, albeit with good intentions, convinces her to embrace life in a different way: eat and live however you want, and forget about the doctor's orders. Essentially, Karen forfeits her long-term goal for short term gratification: indulging in Henry's delicious desserts. Furthermore, it's tempting, because Henry becomes a regular fixture in Karen's life, which makes life more enjoyable in some aspects, though Karen becomes disillusioned with her own progress, once she realized that sacrificing her four-month goal for a quick "fix" only reversed the hard work. In the end, she gained most of the weight loss and had to accept that the goal was not achieved.

What could Karen have done differently? There are a few options she could have explored, including communicating more with Henry about the importance of following her diet and completing the four-month milestone. Building emotional intelligence, along with prolonging or delaying gratification, would effectively give Karen more confidence to communicate clearly and firmly. Henry, on the other hand, could also benefit from developing EQ skills and a better understanding of Karen's situation by observing cues, including her hesitation when offered dessert. Noting her reaction and understanding the importance of weight loss to Karen are indicators for Henry to accommodate Karen's preference for low carb options, and to cease convincing her that the diet is wrong and unnecessary. Overall, Karen can benefit from more assertiveness, while Henry should improve his listening skills.

**Scenario 2:**

Daniel is twenty-five years old and working at a local grocery store in the deli section. He enjoys his job, but it's a stagnant position with no room for advancement, so he decides to apply for college. At the same time, Daniel also applies for a loan and calculates that with a tight, yet manageable budget, he can continue to work slightly fewer hours, attend a veterinarian assistant program and still afford all the bills and rent he shares with his roommate, Stan. Not only is Daniel interested in earning a better salary, he also wants a job where he can connect more with animals. Over the past two years, he volunteered at a local animal shelter, fostering several cats and dogs, which is how his passion for them developed. To begin a path towards this goal, Daniel decides that he must jump into the mindset of the long term and ignore the temporary difficulties he may experience while he struggles financially.

Within a couple of months, Daniel finds out that he is accepted into the veterinarian assistant program and is approved for a loan to cover the cost of the program, but nothing further, which means he will need to work to save a bit more than expected to cover living expenses. The program begins in five months. Daniel finds additional work to make up the difference and successfully saves for the future. The program is two years, which may not be sustained by the extra earnings over the five months, though Daniel is determined to start the program and finish it with honors. A career change is something that he has considered over the past three years of his life, and now is the prime chance to move in a new direction.

Stan, Daniel's roommate, leaves unexpectedly, without advance notice. Daniel struggles to find a new roommate, and in the meantime, he pays the full amount of rent, which is double what he normally spends. A co-worker offers to move in, though not until shortly after the school year begins, which makes it financially more challenging. Despite these setbacks, Daniel is focused on beginning school, and researches grants and additional funding options to keep things afloat when money becomes scarce. With the exception of some help from his dad, who doesn't have much to spare, Daniel begins school and works reduced hours at the grocery store. Shortly after school begins, Daniel's supervisor offers him a promotion to assistant manager. The position is full-time and provides a significant salary increase with medical benefits. Considering his long-term plan of becoming a veterinarian assistant, Daniel is suddenly thrust into a difficult decision-making position. He has just one week to decide. In his mind, the choice is like a "tug-of-war", with each option pulling him with advantages and disadvantages. He decides to use the one week to weigh both as thoroughly as possible so that the final decision is not made in haste:

| College program: Veterinarian's Assistant | | Promotion to Assistant Manager at the grocery store | |
|---|---|---|---|
| Pros | Cons | Pros | Cons |
| A college diploma or degree in a skilled field of work | Reduced work hours and less income to meet daily living expenses | Increase in salary and the addition of medical benefits | Accepting this position would not allow any room for full-time study in a college program |
| Centers around the passion of animals and their care, which is important | The possibility that there is not enough work in animal care for veterinarian assistants, including new college graduates with little or no experience | Working with senior management could lead to future promotions and salary increases | Long-term employment is never a guarantee, even when a position appears solid and long-term. |
| Lack of regret in pursuing a career of passion, and the chance of | Loss of an opportunity to become an assistant manager of a | With a full-time position and salary increase, no roommate would be | The position would not provide the same level of satisfaction as |

| gaining a decent salary in this field. | grocery store. | necessary. There is more financial freedom and means to live with more stability. | achieving a college diploma or degree, and working in a field that fulfills a passion |
| A positive investment in education. | Student loan and less working hours to pay following the completion of the program | | |

As the above table indicates, Daniel came up with a number of pros and cons for each decision, though there is one missing component that he doesn't notice immediately: the impact of aiming for the long-term goal versus settling for the short-term gratification. Thinking on a more EQ level, and taking into consideration his talent and compassion for animals, Daniel considers the following in finalizing his decision:

**<u>Delayed Gratification</u>** = focusing on the end of the two-year college studies, which is the successful completion of the program, and better prospects of gaining employment in a career that pays well and involves a passion for animals and their well-being.

**<u>Short-Term Gratification</u>** = accepting the assistant manager position and dropping out of the college program to satisfy financial instability currently, with little or no plans for the future.

As tempting as it seems, Daniel declines the promotion to assistant manager. He has a long conversation with his boss, explaining the importance of his college education, and his intention of becoming a veterinarian's assistant. Initially, his boss is disappointed, but he continues to listen and pay attention to Daniel's positive intonation, and signs of both excitement and joy in his non-verbal gestures. Acknowledging the risk of this decision, and yet determined to work towards a passionate goal, Daniel earns the respect of his employer and continues to work part-time in the deli. His new roommate moves in, and the college year begins. It will be a struggle over the next two years, though Daniel posts notes and reads inspirational stories to keep his sights on the end of the program, which he eventually completes with a good average and some opportunities that may lead to future prospects.

**Analysis of Scenario 2:**

Daniel's decision was not an easy task. He had two very promising options, both of which could improve his life more than his present situation. When he weighed all the options, the ultimate decision was a college education. Some people in the same or similar situation may not approve, based on the financial difficulty and debt that accompanies a student's life, especially where there is little or no financial support available from family or full paid scholarships. The main point of this scenario was not whether Daniel decided on college or the promotion, but rather how he made the final choice: all options were considered. The time frame of one week, which was provided to Daniel, was utilized wisely, in that he didn't make a quick or hasty decision without considering the consequences. Emotional maturity plays a significant role in taking responsibility or your decisions and making sure you know what you're getting into before you start. In the event where Daniel had a spouse, family, or other commitments to consider, he may have made the opposite decision for the benefit of the situation.

## Scenario 3:

Billy is a risk-taker in life and enjoys everything from traveling to exotic countries to skydiving and mountain climbing. He dedicates a great deal of time and effort into his travels, using a good portion of his income from his full-time job as a fitness instructor to travel as much as possible. When he lived at home with his parents, there was more disposable income to use for travel, though since moving away to another country, Billy had to learn to budget his finances to cover living expenses, while scheduling time off in advance to travel. The prospect of routine and responsibility irritated and frustrated Billy, who would rather travel continuously and avoid the daily grind of regular employment.

When Billy turned thirty-five years old, he realized that he had not accomplished his ultimate dream: to become a stunt actor in a film. Ever since childhood, Billy fantasized about becoming a famous stunt performer. Action films and scenes captivated him, and from a young age, he took physical fitness seriously, joining sports teams and becoming very competitive. In his early teens, he studied martial arts and weight training. His parents were supportive of his hard work, though encouraged him to focus on more career-oriented goals in business and finance, instead of physical fitness and sports, which they felt was too risky and unsustainable. Billy disagreed, and after years of conflict, he moved out of his parents' home and rented a small bachelor, working full time at a gym and completing his certificate as a fitness instructor and personal trainer. It was a good job, and eventually, his parents became comfortable and accepting of the idea, and offered to help him buy a condominium. Upon moving into his new condo, Billy promptly sub-let the unit, and began traveling and working as a personal trainer, sometimes living, or staying at different resorts and venues that were new and exciting. When he finally settled into a full-time training position, he felt that his life became too stagnant, and decided to begin auditioning for film roles.

With little or no experience, Billy didn't get much of a break in the film industry. He traveled where there was an opportunity for more work in film, though this didn't help either. The income from the condominium rental was running low, and his parents refused to give him any further money until he made a responsible decision to either return to full-time employment or enroll in college and pursue business. Billy was annoyed at the idea of abandoning his dreams and continued working different gigs and trying for stunt roles. When he finally landed a couple of small roles on film, he felt accomplished, though far from his goal. Any attempt from his parents to convince him that pursuing stunt work was a bad idea fell on deaf ears. Billy wasn't going to stop, and even in his mid-thirties, where he would encounter more challenges in a youth-centered industry, he refused to give up.

**Analysis of Scenario 3:**

Billy is a passionate and active person, who doesn't mind taking a risk, even if it is at his own or someone else's expense. While steady employment was always available and offered to Billy, he continually chose to avoid it, choosing a less stable life, for the purpose of experiencing the thrill of risk. How does Billy's EQ measure in terms of his emotional maturity and ability to differentiate between delayed gratification and short-term benefits?  On the surface, Billy lives "' in' the moment", and thrives on the notion of swinging from one gig to another, which satisfies his need for instant gratification or satisfying the short-term thrill of a stunt role or equally exciting travel destination or event.  In this way, he doesn't show a high degree of emotional maturity or EQ, because these plans only satisfy the short-term and don't provide a more stable, long-term goal that would eventually bring a higher degree of contentment.

Despite their good intentions, Billy's parents focused too much on giving him rewards, such as offering their home rent-free and buying a condominium, in order to essentially "bribe" him into focusing on a business-related career instead.  This shows a lack of instilling emotional maturity in Billy at a young age, and also, failing to fully support his passions, and instead, convincing him to change his path. Financially, Billy learned to rely heavily on his parents, while embarking on his own journey despite their disagreement.  There is a lack of EQ skills on all sides, and this could improve if each party would weigh the level of responsibility they need and what their decision or actions impact the others.  Key factors to improve the emotional intelligence for everyone involved includes listening and acknowledging all sides of each argument. Disagreements will occur, and that is acceptable, as long as there remain respect and space given to express those thoughts and ideas.  Billy's parents must simply accept that he is not going to take their advice and stop funding his efforts in order to try convincing him to change. On the other hand, Billy must accept the significant risks he takes in chasing the stunt acting work, and acknowledging that while his parents may not agree with his choices, that they make the valid point of highlighting the risk in his work, and must accept it.

Delayed gratification is not an easy path for everyone. We are wired to enjoy the immediate benefits of what we can get now or soon, rather than wait longer for the reward. In the end, a series of short-term rewards will not combine into the satisfaction of accomplishing a long-term goal or achievement. This is done by continuous dedication, self-discipline, and hard work.

## What Steps Can You Take to Delay Gratification?

### To Save or to Spend?

We all know people who love to spend money whenever they have the chance, going on shopping sprees or ordering the newest technology or gadgets with little or no consideration for their budget. There are also people who tend to save every dime and avoid spending as much as possible. While saving is ideal, as it can prepare you for unforeseen expenses and financial well-being in the future, it doesn't have to require absolute avoidance of spending completely. Some people make a point of only spending money on things they need and avoid shopping malls, online shopping, and other venues to keep themselves from being distracted. While this is helpful and positive for their finances, some people may go as far as to restrict themselves from certain items they need for the sake of putting a couple of extra dollars in the bank.

Like most things in life, balance is key. Knowing when to spend versus save can be a good tool to employ when you tend to lean extremely one way or the other. Depriving yourself of healthy food, for example, so that you can save on a grocery bill and buy cheaper, fewer quality goods should be avoided if you have the ability to afford healthy goods. On the other hand, overspending is a chronic problem that many people face, often leading to high credit card debt and in severe cases, bankruptcy. It doesn't "pay" to overspend, and sometimes holding onto every coin isn't the best either.

Switching from chronic spending to saving doesn't happen overnight. Once we become accustomed to spending often, we may find it hard to break the cycle. Simply stopping is akin to quitting an addiction: it takes time and adjustment to change spending habits. Small changes can be an important way to slowly adapt from the "spend" to the "save" mentality:

- When a specific item or store appears in view, take a realistic look at what spending your money will achieve: is it something you need? If it's an item you really want, will you use it often?

- Write down which item(s) you will allow yourself to buy, versus the items that will no longer be purchased. For example, grabbing a fresh coffee or pastry on the go may be practical, though can add up over time. If you decide that it is a worthwhile and enjoyable expense, then review another spending to determine what can be avoided or "trimmed" from the menu of items you shop for. Taking your lunch to work or school, avoiding sales pitches and flyers that may encourage you to spend when you normally wouldn't. Make an effort to control how, when and the amount you spend.

- Track the amount of money you save by not spending it on what you normally would. For example, if you reduce the number of meals you eat at restaurants and buy a few extra groceries instead, calculate the difference between both expenses and add them weekly to determine the amount of your savings. Once this becomes a regular habit, you'll notice a positive trend, with more disposable money to either save or pay towards bills and/or debt.


## Avoid Temptations and Triggers

This is not an easy task and requires sometimes minor or major changes in your routine. For some people, a change in routine to avoid a tempting item could mean taking a different route home from work that doesn't involve passing a shopping mall, in order to avoid shopping and overspending. For other people, this could be avoiding fast food outlets to reduce their intake of convenience foods. If a person is on a diet or making healthier lifestyle choices, avoiding routines or places where they are more likely to purchase unhealthy food is one step. Another option is to stock up on healthier snacks and foods to curb cravings for chips or soda. Food and spending are two major items that provide a lot of pitfalls for people, in terms of how much they spend and the foods they eat. Removing and avoiding the very items that are obstacles in our life is a significant way to improve our rate of success in achieving the long-term goal of saving money, spending less, and/or eating better.

Another major temptation is the addiction to technology. People tend to focus on social media and online means of communication in excess, above and beyond the regular work contacts and connections with other people. With the invention of instant messaging, social media and forums, there is a lot of skewed versions of ourselves and others that we become too involved with, instead of focusing on relationships or goals in real life. Turning the cell phone off for a specific time frame each day and going "tech-free" for a day can be a freeing experience, helping us to reflect on our own thoughts and emotional well-being without any interference.

## Keep Life Simple

Life can get complicated and stressful for anyone. Sometimes we schedule events or plan in advance for weeks or months at a time, and become so involved in multiple tasks and situations, that we rarely take time for ourselves or those close to us. For many people, living a complex life is not a choice, but a necessity, as they may struggle in more ways than one, and have no choice but to continue this way. Simplifying your life doesn't necessarily mean avoiding or shirking responsibility to make life easier, because that is not the best option, nor is it realistic. Keeping life simple can mean scaling back on accumulating too many items, such as collecting and overspending, or avoiding people or situations that create drama and tension when it's completely unwarranted and unnecessary. When there are too many things going on at once, it can be extremely difficult to focus on any goal, long or short term.

## Eat Healthy and Exercise

Maintaining a healthy diet and staying active provides a good foundation for a productive and enjoyable life. This focus on good eating and living is a long-term goal that serves as a practice to embark on other goals in the same way, by avoiding short-lived satisfaction and instead, aiming for the big goal. A healthy lifestyle also gives us more energy and a better mental and physical framework for accomplishing a lot of work. Without adequate energy and endurance, the chance of failure or falling short of your goal becomes a higher risk. Food is fuel, and we need the best quality in order to give our body and mind the best chance of achieving good results.

**Don't Limit Yourself**

Sometimes we place limits on our abilities and achievements, because of what other people say or how we perceive ourselves. When this happens, we dismiss certain goals or aspirations, with the deeply entrenched belief that we are incapable of doing so. When this happens, we basically defeat our plans and goals before we have a chance to begin. Being realistic with our abilities and goals is important, as not everything is within reach, though we tend to set the bar of our talents low, in that even some extraordinary goals can be achieved with the right mindset, plan, and actions. When we underestimate ourselves, it can be due to many factors: negative feedback and criticism from others, what we internalize about our own capabilities and not having the willpower to accomplish what we want. How often do some people, including ourselves, say "I'm not good at this sort of thing, so I won't succeed," or "I'm not cut out for this, there's not a chance I could do it". This form of defeating yourself usually stems from external comments from people or feelings based on them. We tend to internalize a lot of what we hear, even when it's not accurate. Once we become aware of this, and how these internalized thoughts affect our emotions and feelings, we can attempt to move beyond it. Establishing will power is another way of learning the power we can have over our own thoughts and actions.

**Establish a Plan "B"**

Not all goals can be achieved, and sometimes there is a good reason. We may simply run out of funding for a project due to a lack of adequate fundraising or need to abandon a project when a natural disaster or other unforeseen situation occurs. In all cases, despite the level of risk, it's beneficial to establish a backup plan, or plan B to move in a different or similar situation. Sometimes, the backup plan coincides with the original plan, or it may take a completely different course of action. Most people overlook back up plans, as they may have confidence in the project or goal, though there are always situations that can thwart plans. The best plan of action is to always have a "what if" mindset and consider what would happen if plan A doesn't work, then progress to plan B, with possible third or fourth options. Contingency or back up planning can be valuable in emergency situations as well, where one catastrophic event can impact many people at once. A fire safety or evacuation plan is one example, and often includes alternative meeting places, such as a local community center or facility, in the event the regular venue or place becomes unavailable.

Planning for disasters is a major example, though on a smaller scale, making alternative plans in case the initial project doesn't work, is always a wise method of making sure one plan eventually moves ahead, which increases the chances of succeeding.

**Focus on Anticipation**

Anticipation is a strong and valuable tool for focusing on the long haul. Working towards a major accomplishment can take anywhere from several months to years to fulfill completely. It can be difficult and challenging to see the finish line when you're near the beginning or halfway through. When this happens, people often become discouraged and give up, or try to take short cuts, which may cause more harm and delay the progress. Focusing on the final destination is where anticipation becomes important. Visualize your success, and make it a focal point of your thoughts, which can help anchor you from start to finish.

**Allow Forgiveness**

We all make mistakes, and sometimes just one minor change or wrong turn can derail months or years of hard work and accomplishment. When this happens, we can become angry with ourselves, and blame ourselves or others for the failure. It can lead to conflict and lower the chances of starting over. When we experience agitation and frustration internally, and may or may not express it, and instead we hold onto blame which only causes negative feelings about the entire experience. Some people are plagued with perfectionism and become disappointed even when insignificant items are not exact. One of the most empowering and important steps to take in these instances is twofold: acknowledge the error and forgive yourself. When we acknowledge, we don't have to search for an alternative solution or plan right away. Take time to console your mind and take comfort in the level of effort you contributed, as this is the most important aspect of the learning process.

In learning to understand the significance of our failures or mistakes, we need to learn to forgive and move on. This is another way of understanding the long-term process of delayed gratification. On that long road, there will often be plenty of mistakes to learn from, which should never be dwelt upon for too long, but reflected upon for improvement in the future.

# Learning Self-Discipline and Impulse Control

Self-discipline and impulse control are important for establishing a successful life in many ways, including mastering a good command of emotional intelligence. Learning self-discipline is an acquired skill that requires a lot of self-assessment and reflection. It requires that we get to who we are well before we can work on improving impulse control. The following steps are the foundation for building a successful life based on self-discipline and working towards achieving personal, social, and professional goals:

1. **What are your Weaknesses?** We all have them, even if we convince ourselves that we don't. Job interviews often ask us what our weaknesses are, which may cause you to hesitate and come up with a quick response, without much thought given to why we are asked. Knowing what your weaknesses are is an important trait required for achieving emotional intelligence. By knowing and admitting to having weaknesses, we show that we are mature enough to acknowledge them and work with or around them. Weaknesses are often characteristics that can be improved upon over time and describing them as such is a positive way to understand and express their value.

2. **Recognize Old Habits and Building New, More Productive Habits.** Not all habits are negative, though some may hinder our success. Before we can plan or work towards achieving a goal, recognizing which habits we have are advantageous and which ones are harmful, can help us install some new changes in our lives that provide a new, pivotal point where we can begin. An example of a negative

habit, though very common, is procrastination. Many people simply put off what they cannot do at the moment, though procrastination is often done to avoid starting a project or completing it. There are many reasons that people put off doing things; a lack of confidence in their ability to complete a task, the fear of failure, and simply not wanting to do it. Not all tasks are pleasant or easy, though they are necessary. Paying bills, completing an essay or homework project or chores at home can seem unfulfilling and boring. The importance of achieving these tasks in a timely manner is one way to establish self-discipline. Create a schedule to get tasks done and stick with the time frames. To start, allow for some flexibility in the schedule, in case you get busy and need to shift certain items, for example, from morning to afternoon. Building new, more productive habits may include keeping a log of your daily activities and progress on a specific project or goal. Setting smaller milestones to make the overall goal seem less difficult and more achievable, on a step-by-step basis, is another way to maintain interest while staying on track.

3. **Document Your Progress**. Keep a diary or note pad of all the steps taken towards achieving the project and goals you set to achieve. This can provide a sense of accomplishment, and help you visualize the plan as it develops. In many cases, people will review previous notes as a checklist, to make sure they didn't miss any steps and remain on the right track. Maintaining a log doesn't have to be an exhausting task of including a lot of description and detail. It can be simple,

which one or two sentences for each day or block of time set aside for the project.

4. **Don't Compare Yourself to Others.** Focus on you and your goals. If the project involves a team, work with each other instead of against. We often get caught in the habit of comparing our achievements (or lack thereof) with other people, which isn't realistic nor is it fair. Not everyone has the same resources or options, depending on their circumstances. We all have different levels of talent across of wide spectrum of abilities, and there will always be someone who is "better" than us at one task or another. What matters most, in our personal life, is that we focus on self-improvement and compete against one person only: ourselves.

Improving self-discipline and impulse control are ongoing and lifelong goals for most people. Making changes, such as new habits and practices that help with progression towards a stronger level of emotional intelligence and control over your life. As this improves, life only gets better with more possibilities and opportunities.

# Chapter Four: Developing Language Skills for Better Communication and Empathy

## Using Language (Verbal and Non-verbal) to Improve Social EQ Skills (intonation in speech, talking speed and style, what to look for in non-verbal communication)

The way we communicate and speak to other people can make a significant difference in how we react emotionally. It's not just what we say, but how we speak. Tone and timing can make the difference between a sarcastic comment and a more serious one. We might make a comment or statement the wrong way, depending on our perception of it, and some people are better at conveying their true feelings and expressions than others. This chapter looks at how different levels of tone, talking speed and style of speech can have an impact on communication and empathy. Non-verbal communication and gestures also apply, as many people use non-speaking cues to show their true feelings.

### Intonation Used in Speech

Intonation, when used in speech, is defined as the pitch or tone of speaking. It can refer to singing or speech during a conversation or discussion. People use various tones to emphasize their emotions in their thoughts and words. There are different types of intonation, and all of them have an effect on how speech is heard and understood. The speaker may or may not even be aware of the effect their intonation has on the listener, while sometimes they may purposely use specific tones or a combination of tone to achieve a specific effect. The various patterns of intonation are as follows:

The increase in tone or pitch at the end of a sentence: this is otherwise known as a question. In nearly every question we are asked or ask, we emphasize the purpose of the statement, to ask the question, by increasing the pitch at the end. Most people understand this as a question without further explanation:

"Can you help me with some <u>directions?</u>" – the change in pitch occurs on "directions"

"What time <u>is it?</u>" – the word "time" may be emphasized, as it is the subject in question, though the tone increases higher in pitch with "is it"?

The opposite of raising pitch is known as a "falling pitch". This occurs when the pitch falls towards the end of the sentence. It's effective in making a definitive statement that you feel confident is accurate and correct, such as the following examples:

"I'm <u>certain</u> they will be here in <u>one hour</u>." – the word "certain" is emphasized, whereas the words that follow gradually decline in pitch or "fall", with the words "one hour" being the lowest pitch or sound.

"The train leaves once an hour on the <u>half-hour</u>." – this is another definitive statement, where the subject of discussion, "train" has the strongest sound or emphasis, and the pitch gradually declines until it reaches its lowest at "half-hour"

Intonation can fall, then rise, or rise, then fall, when a statement indicates a situation or event that has occurred, though may change in the future. Sometimes this method the changing pitch from high to low or vice versa is used to ask questions in a more pleasant tone:

"Are these your folders?" the word "is" is neutral, where "these" and "folders" are raised in pitch. The up-and-down intonation technique of this question usually makes an impression that the person asking is polite and cautious about asking.

"May I have a glass of water?" this question is asking for an item, which can come across as demanding, if the tone is minimal in change, almost monotone (with little or no intonation), or it can sound more pleasing if "I", "glass" and "water" are raised in pitch, creating a rise and fall effect throughout the sentence.

Intonation is just one method that speech can change our perception by simply changing the sound of the pitch without altering the words. It can make the difference between sounding rude and mean to appear politer. When we perceive someone as polite, we have a favorable impression of them and may perceive them as kind and sincere, whereas low or no intonation can have the effect of making a person appear angry or sad.

## Talking Speed

How quickly or slow we speak can make a major impact on how we are perceived by others, and how they view our emotions. The most neutral way to speak is to keep your speech evenly spaced, speaking neither too fast nor too slow. Moving towards one extreme or another may convey certain impressions that may or may not be accurate about a person and how they are expressing themselves.

Speaking quickly can denote many different things. For example, if a person continually stumbles over their words and speaks too quickly, they may be very nervous or anxious. This may be due to the person or people they are talking to, who they may feel uneasy with, or the subject matter they are discussing. If a person comes across as nervous or anxious, they may seem as in a panic and not taken too seriously, unless their speech becomes more erratic, or urgent, which may indicate an emergency situation and a state of shock.

For some people, speaking quickly is done when they feel the need to get out as much information as possible within a small window of time. Some people perceive speaking quickly and concisely as a sign of high intelligence, as their mind is thinking quickly along with their speech. The problem with speaking too quickly is how it can be difficult to understand the speaker, and they often have to be asked to slow down and repeat certain passages for clarification. In a world connected to technology, we have become accustomed to instant messaging and the need for an immediate answer to everything at once. When this happens, we tend to adapt by quickening our speech to match, though it becomes ineffective and hard to understand by the average person.

Other drawbacks to speaking too quickly include appearing insensitive or aggressive, even when you keep your pace consistent. It can also give the impression that you lack empathy or consideration for others, as you appear to be rushing through the conversation instead of pausing for a response or failing to actively engage with others. When this negative impression is established, it can make it more challenging to continue speaking with the person or people involved, as they will become discouraged by the unwanted speech pattern and lose interest. The message you wish to convey can also become lost, and any point you want to make becomes unimportant to listeners.

Speaking slowly can be helpful in communicating with people who have a language barrier, as they often observe the non-verbal cues along with the speech. It can also be ideal for people who learn at a different pace and can benefit from hearing speech annunciated slowly, accurately and with a consistent rhythm. In these cases, communication is strong and both parties can make a better sense of what the other person means when they are speaking. In adjusting your speech to a slower pace for certain people and circumstances, it shows a degree of EQ, in that you are aware of someone else's struggle to understand, empathize with them and make an effort to adjust your communication to accommodate.

When speaking slowly becomes too slow, it can make a listener feel as though they are not considered intelligent enough to understand a more moderate pace. This can have the effect of making some people feel as though they are being "talked down to", berated or patronized. When this happens, the reaction may be negative in response, such as "do you think I'm stupid?" or "I know, you don't have to explain it to me like a small child."

When communicating verbally, keeping your speech intonation natural and speed moderate, you'll avoid a lot of misperceptions from people who may be interested in what you have to say, and will pay more attention if the speech is pleasant and easy to comprehend. The following tips are good to put into practice for all forms of conversation:

- Make use of pausing. It indicates that you are giving the other person a chance to say something or contribute to the discussion. It also gives you a chance to take a quick break and simply let the other person absorb what's been said so far. Pausing should be brief after each comma, and slightly longer at the end of a sentence. The longer pause should be reserved after a point of view or issue has been completely expressed, usually in several sentences.

- If you need to call out a list of people's names or items, avoid rushing through them, making sure to pronounce each item or name clearly and slowly. It's a good idea to slow down considerably, as some names may be hard to pronounce, and can also be spelled for clarification. This avoids misunderstanding and negative responses from someone hearing their name mispronounced.

- If you feel that you are not being clearly understood, ask your audience. If anyone is unhappy about the speed of talking, they will make it clear at that time. This gives you a chance to "redeem" yourself from a possible negative impression of not being properly understood. The most common complaint people usually have concerning speech is speaking too quickly and not loudly enough. Keeping this in mind, make sure to speak loud clear and not too fast, and most issues with understanding are usually avoided.

## Talking Style

There are many different speaking styles that incorporate various speeds and intonation in each, such as descriptive speaking, conversations that engage others and educational lectures. All of these and other styles have a specific purpose and level of importance for their audience. In all cases, loud and clear speech is the best way to get the information and message across. Without clarify, it doesn't matter how important the lecture is or how informative a person may be, they will not accurately convey their thoughts. There are some additional habits or practices that should be avoided when speaking to one or more people, including before an audience:

- Avoid interruptions. If someone is speaking, give them the space to do so and wait until they are finished a complete thought or item. During this stage, they will pause, which gives another person an opportunity to contribute to the discussion. Interrupting someone is not only rude and inconsiderate, but it can also cause them to lose their train of thought. When this happens, they may not want to communicate at all or become visibly irritated. If you find interrupting has become a bad habit, apologize immediately and work towards eliminating it altogether

- Changing topics frequently. Switching the topic of conversation happens when one subject has concluded, and another, more interested or relevant item is introduced into the discussion. It can simply be part of a speech before an audience, where the next chapter or section in a seminar requires changing the topic to continue. When subjects are changed too frequently and without warning, it can have the same impact or impression on someone as interrupting: it appears rude and thoughtless. This is especially upsetting if a conversation concerning a specific topic is very engaging and several people are enjoying a civilized discussion or debate. When one person unexpectedly introduces a new topic, it's disrespectful. If a topic of conversation is contentious or difficult to participate in, it's perfectly acceptable to politely excuse yourself from the conversation and return later.

- Using overly descriptive words and fancy terms when it's not necessary. People often do this to impress others, and it shows. They often do this with the idea that using a fancier or more complex sounding word is somehow more impressive and will garner more respect and attention than the simpler, or "boring" term. One major drawback of using fancier terms when unnecessary is making a simple topic appear more complex than it is. This may cause confusion and people tend to back away from the discussion altogether. Another drawback is using words in the wrong context. This can be embarrassing for the speaker and ruin their credibility. Unless a speech or discussion warrants very specific terms that happen to be complex, such as scientific terms, it's best to stick with the most direct words, which may seem boring, but not if your overall speech pattern has good speed and intonation.

- Drawn out talking and overdone descriptions. Keep your talking clear and concise as much as possible. Descriptions are helpful, but they should not become so detailed and drawn out that people lose interest. Imagine reading a novel where the plot became stagnant or slowed done because of over-descriptions of scenes and simple, daily tasks for page after page. This would prompt most readers to stop or at the very least, reconsider continuing the book. Keep this in mind when describing a person, place, or item to someone; keep it direct and relevant, so that they stay interested.

Investing the time and effort to improve how we communicate with others is a major component of improving emotional intelligence. It means that we value other people's time and interest, so that speaking is direct and intentional, avoiding misunderstandings and miscommunication as much as possible.

## Body Language and Observation: How to Adapt to Your Environment and Adjust your EQ Skill Success

Applying body language techniques is just as important as observing and understanding other people's body language and non-verbal communication. Learning to recognize non-verbal cues and what they mean to give us a good indication of what another person is thinking or trying to convey. Sometimes these cues are used on their own, or in conjunction with verbal communication. If a person feels uncomfortable expressing how they feel, for example, they may not say anything, or speak in constant to their inner thoughts. This section will cover how a person with a high EQ skill set will adapt in different situations successfully, and how non-verbal cues and gestures can be observed and used to communicate effectively.

People with high EQ have a lot of beneficial traits that either come naturally or developed and improved over time. They utilize observation as a primary indicator of how other people may be reacting to them or other immediate situations that impact them. In observing others and the environment around them, people show their strong EQ skills with the following reflections and actions in how they interact with others:

- They are aware of their comfort zone, and when they are moving in and out of it. Some people refer to "stepping outside of their comfort zone" when they try something new or go out on a date with someone new. For people with strong emotional intelligence, they are more in tune and aware of when they venture outside of their own comfort zone, even slightly. They are also more aware and accepting of their vulnerabilities than other people, and willing to step outside of that comfort zone in order to gain a better understanding and connection with other people

- A willingness to consider different viewpoints. This is one of the classic traits of a person with a good EQ level, who not only solicits the idea of a contrary viewpoint to their own but wants to truly understand why someone else would support it. This can be difficult territory when the subject is controversial or contentious in nature, though a person with emotional maturity will strive more for understanding than debate.

- They take everything in stride. They may be negatively impacted emotionally when someone insults them or treats them unfairly, though they are slow to react. A person with high EQ will weigh the options of responding or reacting quickly versus taking time to respond. They see the value in constructive criticism and use it to make improvements as needed.

- They are patient. People with strong EQ skills value patience, as it is within this time frame that they utilize to make a thoughtful decision or plan an appropriate approach or response. When experiencing a setback, they use it as an opportunity to try harder next time and avoid thinking negatively about it.

- Positive people have negative feelings, and it's completely natural to experience both, even for someone who is emotionally mature. When you feel negative, it's important to acknowledge it and find the source of the emotion. It could be simply due to a stressful day, or another more serious event that may take time to adjust to. In all cases, acknowledging any type of negativity and understanding that it is a natural occurrence is important.

- They understand non-verbal cues. A significant benefit of people with high EQ is the ability to read and understand other people's non-verbal gestures and cues. The next section will further discuss the impact and importance of reading other people's cues and signs that indicate what they are truly feeling.

## Non-Verbal Cues and Communication

We are likely familiar with many forms of non-verbal communication including common gestures and signals we use ourselves in an everyday situation. Some of the most common forms of non-verbal communication include nodding of the head, to show agreement and say "yes", or shaking the head side-to-side to show disagreement or say "no". A "thumbs up" means acceptance or a positive agreement, whereas folding your arms across your chest indicates that you are closed to a certain person or situation, or simply keeping your guard up in an uncertain situation. The main forms of non-verbal communication and examples of each are as follows:

## Making Eye Contact

This is a common way to read people when we communicate with them. When eye contact is established and maintained, it means we have someone's complete attention. They are paying attention to us and listening to what we have to say. On the other hand, when they divert contact and look away, or easily drift to other people or items, it can indicate that they are disinterested or bored with the conversation. They may not realize that they are drifting away, or they may use this gesture to communicate their dislike or lack of interest in us. Sometimes, a person's eyes may blink a lot when they are nervous or agitated. They may roll their eyes when they are humored or slightly annoyed at a comment. When someone closes their eyes momentarily, it may be to savor a delicious mouthful of a tasty dessert or to reflect on something on a more serious level, which is internal and personal.

## Body Posture

The way a person stands, sits or poses can say a lot about what is on their mind. When someone stands tall and firm, with their hands by their sides, they are showing a strong degree of confidence and openness. With their hands-free, they can easily shake hands or provide an embrace. This position is a good posture in business or when meeting someone for the first time. It gives a good impression of confidence, balanced with comfort. When someone folds their arms, either sitting or standing, they may be hesitant or feel intimidated by a person or situation. They may also wish to remain guarded, and not express too much about themselves until they are ready. A curved positive indicates a lack of comfort and confidence. It can also be an indication of shyness or feeling intimidated.

## Distance and Closeness

People will keep their distance in situations that they are unsure of, and maintain the distance until they are comfortable. On the other hand, some people move in very close to appearing engaged, though this can cause some people to feel uncomfortable, as it may be seen as an invasion of personal space. Maintaining a distance that is neither near nor far is best because it allows someone to hold your attention, without getting too close for comfort or too far for effective communication. Remaining arms-length or slightly closer shows the other person that you are interested in conversing or engaging with them.

## Facial Expressions showing Feelings

As common as facial expressions are, we often don't think about our own expressions as well as see others. For example, we may be deep in thought, only to have someone ask us if anything is wrong due to a sad or stoic expression. We might suddenly smile when thinking of a funny joke, though no one else will understand it. Other facial expressions include shock, fear, disgust, frustration, anger, and sadness. We might have a slightly different way of smiling when we are happy than the next person, though it's easily recognizable as contentment.

## Hand and Body Gestures

There are many different hand, finger and body gestures that communicate specific meanings and messages. Depending on the culture or region, some gestures can be seen as either offensive or friendly.

# Chapter Five: Building Social Relationships

## Keys to Developing Better Social Relationships

Developing and improving our relationships with people is a key method of improving our emotional intelligence. It also gives us more of an opportunity to improve relationships we already have with friends, family, neighbors, and co-workers. There will always be challenges, considering the different personalities and conflicts we have with them. Sometimes overreacting or acting on impulse is how we may respond to situations, without considering the outcome. There are some key methods of building social relationships with others, despite how little or well we know them.

## Always Listen

People want to be heard and understood. When we don't agree with them or understand their point of view, it's still important that we actively listen, and make a point of showing our interest. This gives them a platform to explain, debate, describe or provide information that could ultimately change our perspective to a degree, and broaden our understanding.

## Acknowledge Differences and Similarities

When we relate to someone, we may share a lot in common. There will also be significant differences that may seem to hinder a possible relationship or pose conflict at some point. It's up to us to learn to accept the differences and acknowledge them. This doesn't mean that we have to agree with everything about the other person, though we can recognize and respect their opinions and beliefs as different than ours. When we do this, it creates the expectation of acceptance, tolerance, and respect, all of which are important in friendship and a relationship. It also makes celebrating what we share in common, more enjoyable and rewarding.

## Be in the Present

Give your time to be there for them. Focus on the present, without dwelling on the past or what may happen in the future. The most important time is now and giving your full attention. We often become easily distracted when there are a lot of expectations in our lives, and technology plays a significant role in this as well. We often multitask and try to figure out ways to get more than one item done at once. Often, our personal relationships suffer as a result, because even when we are physically available, our mind isn't, and when we communicate online, it takes minimal time to send a message or ask a few questions. However, when we make a point of setting aside time in person, we put the cell phone away and communicate directly and fully. Giving our full attention is one of the most important ways of becoming good listeners as well. By making our time and attention available to someone, we are telling them that they are important to us and we value them.

## Developing Good Communication Skills

When we think of communication, we may simply think of how we talk to someone, then assume they understand completely what we mean without further explanation. Communication goes beyond the conversation and extends to all forms of verbal and non-verbal engagement. A person may initially agree with a statement by saying "yes" or "I agree", and yet their body language or facial expression may show a different reaction. Being honest and straight forward are the most effective ways to be heard and understood from the start. When we try to dodge a question or hide our true feelings, it can show in other gestures or cues that conflict with what we say. If we feel that someone isn't being clear with their communication, not only is it confusing, it may indicate a sign of dishonesty and inconsistency. This is an important sign to look out for, especially if you plan to share and entrust someone with a great deal of personal information. When we discover that someone isn't the same person that they portray to be, we can feel tricked or misled, which leads to difficulty in trusting other people overall. Always be upfront and say what you mean, so that the other person or people have a clear picture of the message and information behind it.

## Learn to Trust

Some people have more challenges trusting another person, while other people are too trusting too soon. Trusting someone means giving them a chance to be the person they portray to be. If they are consistent, kind and give you no reason to doubt them, over time, you may develop a strong level of trust. This means you will trust them with more information about yourself and they may, in turn, do the same. Honoring someone else's trust in them means being loyal to them. For example, if they relate a very personal detail or situation that they clearly state is confidential, then it's important to respect and maintain that confidentiality. If you are the type of person who is quick to trust someone, take a step back and do a quick check of how well you know them. Giving a small amount of trust can be a test, and a good idea, in the beginning, though exercise caution with how much you give of yourself, before extending that level of trust further.

## Keep the Relationship Positive

When a relationship is positive, this doesn't mean that there are no struggles or conflicts at all, but rather both parties are willing to compromise and rise above their differences when they cause friction. This is especially important when someone is going through a challenging event in life, such as a tragedy or loss. We simply cannot erase their sense of loss or become the immediate solution, though we can remain a positive fixture in their life by being present and lending an ear when they need to talk. Sometimes when people do not feel like talking, they just want to know that you are available for them. Giving them reassurance that you are there for them provides a strong level of comfort in difficult times. In general, remaining positive means avoiding too much complaining and keeping criticism minimal, if necessary. If a friend or colleague asks for an honest opinion, give it to them, but make it constructive as much as possible.

Relationships do not develop instantly. It takes time, sometimes years to foster a meaningful connection with someone. In reality, we may only remain as acquaintances or meet occasionally at certain gatherings, while in other instances, we may develop a stronger bond and develop a relationship over a long period of time. If a person is hesitant to communicate or acts evasive, this may be a sign that developing a relationship may be too challenging, or they simply may not be interested in doing. When we develop relationships with the people we work with or have to deal with on a regular basis, we may not necessarily choose them as friends, if they are not willing to build a social relationship, though building a good level of communication and listening skills can go a long way to making our experience with them more positive.

## Learning to Master Assertiveness

Assertiveness is defined as having the ability to communicate in a way that is confident, by standing up for yourself or another person and doing so in a positive, yet firm manner. It's not the same as aggressiveness, as assertive doesn't aim to intimidate, ignite an angry response, or become reactionary. It's often a well thought out comment or statement that commands respect while giving respect in the process. Being assertive is not the easiest skill to master, as many people lack confidence in confronting a person, people, or situation where they need to speak up in their own defense. One example of assertiveness is when a child faces a bully on the school playground to confront them. If they act aggressively in their confrontation, they might exchange insults with the bully, and push or shove them. They may retaliate and justify the behavior because the bully did it to them first. Assertiveness is different, in that it doesn't involve aggression. Anger is left out of the equation, and what is left is a strongly delivered response, such as "leave me alone, or I'm going to take further action". Further action could mean getting someone else to intervene and prevent future occurrences of bullying, or by standing up for yourself, and stating that you're simply not going to tolerate their behavior anymore, they may back down. Bullies tend to prey on people who appear passive and lack confidence.

How do we go from being passive and not assertive enough, or too aggressive to assertive? When we are subjected to humiliation or undermined in a specific circumstance, we may try to avoid confronting the person or people responsible, in order to avoid further mistreatment or lose our temper and give them a piece of our mind. When either of these options is used, it only makes the situation worse, and we may still be subjected to more of the same again. Being assertive means balancing the bluntness of aggression with the softness of passiveness with a firm, well-delivered message that we are not going to tolerate disrespect or mistreatment of any kind. The following steps are important in establishing assertiveness:

1. Be direct and state your concerns without laying any blame or accusations. Make a point of respecting other people's rights at that moment, while asserting that they should respect yours.

2. Keep your statement or response brief and simple. Make your point clear and incontestable. When this is done, you will notice people stand up and take notice. It is known as a "no-nonsense" approach. It can also be effective in putting the onus on the other person to own up to their actions and explain them, especially if their mistreatment of you and other people is commonly known.

3. Focus on problem-solving as the main goal. Assertiveness is more than a confrontation or standing up for yourself; it requests that the behavior causing the grief stops altogether. Vocalize your expectations, and do so carefully, based on the environment you are in. For example, following a statement of "I'm not going to tolerate your disrespect of me and/or other people" may be added with "What can I (or we) expect from you going forward? How can we communicate in a way that is effective, productive, while maintaining respect?" This will facilitate the next step, which is to use your assertiveness

to change the course of action and behavior so that the environment becomes more positive

4. Adapt to each situation with an appropriate response. Assertiveness is not always an accepted method in some places of employment, where the customer is a priority, even where the employee is at the receiving end of an abusive statement or action. In some regions and countries, there are laws that protect people, especially employees, from discrimination and harassment, however, in many cases, the mistreatment or offense doesn't necessarily fit into any of these categories. In some incidences, employers will side with the client or customer over the employee, which makes showing any sign of assertiveness towards the customer impossible. When this happens, focus your attention on the supervisor or employer instead. Arrange to meet with them in private or separately and address your concerns. Ensure that you prepare in advance, so that what you state and how you say it is well rehearsed and can be stated with as much confidence as possible.

5. Avoid hesitation and procrastination, wherever possible. This means addressing a situation right away so that it is taken seriously and handled sooner. Being assertive at a moment's notice can take practice, as our first instinct may be to avoid responding altogether or to become reactionary or aggressive. Unless it is unavailable to confront someone right away, do so as soon as possible; make your voice heard and begin the process of improving communication and establishing expectations of more respect.

6. When people become more assertive, they don't appear as victims, but rather, as empowered individuals who are not afraid to confront someone who mistreats them. Some people may visualize this as moving from "victim" to "survivor" in serious cases where a person faces someone who has caused them injury. It can be a frightening, yet powerful experience.

The qualities of assertive people are positive, in that they are looking to build something productive out of a situation by using their voice as a means of doing so. When someone asserts themselves, they are stating the following:

- I am deserving of respect, just as you and everyone else
- I'm not going to play victim, but I won't tolerate your mistreatment of me (and other people)
- Let's work together instead of fighting against each other. This project is a team effort that requires all of us to work together, not apart
- Personal insults will not be tolerated. If you disagree with something I say or do, please state this, instead of taking it out on me personally.
- Let's resolve this problem together

Developing assertiveness improves your EQ level so that you are at a better level of understanding and empathizing with others in the same or similar situation. When other people notice your assertiveness, it can have a very positive effect, encouraging them to respond in kind. When we stand up for other people, who may not have the same voice or ability to do so on their own, this indicates strong compassion and consideration for them.

# Empathy and Good Listening Skills: How to Tap into your Empathetic Nature and Become a Good Listener

Listening to other people is often just as important, if not more vital than how we communicate with them. When someone notices a good listener and detects genuine interest, it gives them a sense that what they have to say is important, and they will be encouraged to relate more to you because of it. Developing good listening skills and taking an interest in someone else is empathetic, as it shows we care and want to hear and understand what the other person has to say. Developing empathy goes hand in hand with improving listening skills, and by developing our empathy, we naturally become better listeners:

- Switch off your tech. Give your full attention and minimize any distractions, including cell phones, other people, and busy places so that you can "tune in" better

- Ask questions. This shows that you have been listening and want to know more. It gives the other person a good opportunity to communicate more openly if they choose to do so.

- Use non-verbal cues to show you are paying attention: nod, focus your eye contact and move closer to them if it is comfortable to do so

- Wait for the other person to pause or stop before responding. This gives them a chance to keep their thoughts on track while you interact with them. If you speak too soon or interrupt, this can cause them to become flustered, confused, and unable to stay consistent. This is especially important when someone is discussing a very personal or delicate manner that requires active listening and understanding.

# Chapter Six: Tips for Improving your EQ Skillset

## Tips for Challenges and Success in Developing your EQ Skillset

Succeeding with the improvement and development of resourceful and helpful EQ skills is essential in becoming more aware of how we interact with people and understand them. When we are aware of other people's emotions, reactions and what they expect, we learn to communicate more effectively and effectively make a better connection with them. The following tips are a summary of how we can foster better skills to achieve a higher level of emotional intelligence:

- Observe people and take note of how they behave around certain people and situations. This will give us a good indication of how we can engage with them and communicate more effectively

- Listen well and carefully. Give your undivided attention and show the other person you are actively listening.

- Take other people seriously, even if they frequently change their minds or go off-topic. Remind them that you are listening and want to know more about (specific topic) so that you can understand them better.

# FAQs

The following frequently asked questions can be helpful in specific situations where the usual solution or answer isn't always the best option. Some situations require a more individual assessment to gauge the best course of action. In some instances, we will make the mistake of reacting too soon or making a bad decision, though, on the other hand, it can serve as a valuable learning experience.

**Q:** What happens if I react in a way that I regret later? I yelled at someone for not doing their job correctly, and now they won't speak with me. I'm their supervisor, but I didn't mean to sound angry or make the situation worse. How can I correct the problem?

**A:** First, accept that the initial approach was not the best idea, and try to reconcile with the employee by inviting them to converse with you in private. If they were reprimanded in front of other people, they may have felt ashamed or embarrassed. Give them an opportunity to discuss the matter, as well as any other concerns they may have. Focus on resolving this situation as a first step, so that the relationship of understanding and positive communication can be re-established. Once this is done, the second step is to discuss performance issues in a constructive manner, so that any issues can be tackled and resolved together. When a person feels targeted, they may become defensive and unwilling to make a compromise. There is always room to improve the relationship, especially when all people involved are willing to talk it out and work towards a better understanding.

**Q:** If I plan to give constructive criticism, what is the best way to do this without causing someone to take offense and become angry with me, while still getting my point(s) across?

**A:** Giving someone constructive criticism is not an easy task. We may experience being on the receiving end of it, though when we are in a position where we are the one to provide constructive criticism. It can be a stressful situation, especially if we are not used to it. One major factor to consider is this: what you say is less important than how you say it. There are several techniques that can help make the experience easier and positive:

Employ diplomacy and timing, so that the environment is calm and stable. Agree to a specific time and place to meet, and minimize distractions so that the focus can be one the conversation

Begin with a compliment or by expressing a positive attribute about the person, before explaining the need for improvement or more effort in a specific area. For example, you may praise an employee for preparing excellent reports with relevant details, followed by addressing the concerns about missing deadlines and developing a plan to get them back on track. In conclusion, you can complement them on another strength, so that the entire conversation doesn't seem too focused on their struggle with meeting deadlines, though they now understand the seriousness of making more of an effort in the future

Don't make it personal. Focus on the issue(s), and if possible, reiterate positive characteristics about them to show that you appreciate their efforts and talents, while requiring more from them.

Offer suggestions and recommendations. When people strive towards self-improvement, they will be more receptive to resources that help them make positive changes.

Use a positive tone. Keep the intonation light and upbeat, so that the conversation remains constructive. If you become focused on simply listing all of the issues or concerns without any positive reinforcement, your statements will not be heard or accepted.

Stick with facts and say only what is needed. Going into too much detail can confuse some people and make them feel inadequate because they don't understand. Keeping it simple and direct as much as possible is the best approach.

**Q:** How do I handle a person who is not empathetic at all, and doesn't want to communicate in a positive manner?

**A:** If possible, avoid them as much as possible, and only communicate minimally and directly when needed. We often can't choose the people we work or live with and learning to deal with very challenging or abrasive personalities can be a testing process. If someone isn't fond of communicating at all, make a point of only speaking to them when it's necessary.

**Q:** Is EQ (emotional intelligence) more successful in people who naturally have high skills and emotional maturity, or can this be achieved in the same way through practice and implementing methods outlined in this book?

**A:** Emotional intelligence is more challenging for some people than others, especially if EQ skills don't come naturally to them. This can serve as a major advantage for people who naturally have high EQ, as it may seem effortless for them, while others must work towards it. There are other factors to consider: how we are were raised as children, how we adapt to different people and respond to them. A person with little or no EQ skill can achieve a lot through the use of observation, which can take time, though it can be just as effective for them as people who appear to be "born" with it.

**Q:** What is the difference between EQ and IQ? Why is it important at work and in everyday life?

**A:** IQ measures cognitive abilities, such as thinking, problem-solving and reasoning. EQ, on the other hand, measures how people interact and behave with others. EQ is also known as "soft skills" or "social savvy". Over the past few decades, employers focus more of their attention on their employees' soft skill set, and in some cases, just as much as they do their practical experience and education. This is particularly important in customer service positions or where people are often meeting with prospective or regular clients. In a more practical, daily application, EQ skills basically help people communicate better with others. They are less likely to engage in conflict unless it is a civilized debate or constructive discussion.

At one time, all or most of the focus was placed on a person's IQ score, which only measures one type of intelligence. There are many people who may score moderately on an IQ test, though high on the EQ scale. While IQ is valuable and well respected, it's also confined and limiting in that it isn't always practical in daily interactions and activities, which is where EQ becomes more relevant.

**Q:** How can EQ skills improve family relations and strained relationships?

**A:** Dealing with family can be rewarding and challenging at the same time. It can take a lot of effort just to be heard or listened to, especially when someone who is familiar with you may assume that they know what you are going to say. Interruptions are usually common, as well as judgmental comments. When this happens, know when to stop, and approach each conversation with the expectation that you will not likely be understood until you are fully listened to. Sometimes a neutral party, such as a mutual family friend or neighbor can offer to mediate and weigh each side of the discussion. This is very useful especially when family disputes are ongoing and without a resolution in sight. Another way to deal with difficult family members is to simply state that you will not engage in any conversation unless you are shown respect. This is a completely logical and appropriate way to handle people who want to cause a stir for no better reason than creating drama. Always steer clear of getting involved in drama or taking sides, unless there is a good, solid reason to do so.

**Q:** Do men have higher EQ than women or are it women that have higher EQ?

**A:** Many studies and results indicate that EQ is relatively equal across the board, where there is not a significant difference between men and women when it comes to EQ levels. Some specific skills may be more likely in men, while others are more prominent in women, though these results vary from one study to the next.

**Q:** Are there EQ tests that I can take to determine my level?

**A:** There are several types of tests available, with the most recognized tests conducted by professionals in the field, who usually charge a fee for the service. There are also some online quizzes and mini-tests that can give you some good indications of whether your EQ is heading in the right direction. The advantage of and EQ test is that there is always room for improvement. A lower score today could evolve into an improved score over months or a year.

**Q:** Can improving EQ skills make me a happier person in life?

**A:** Yes. Increasing your EQ level makes life more fulfilling because we learn to relate and communicate with a much wider audience. When we can communicate and understand people from their own perspectives, instead of only seeing every viewpoint from our own, it can increase our empathy towards others as well. Getting along better with other people has a very positive effect, which makes us more content overall.

**Q:** Does EQ increase with age?

**A:** Not necessarily, though as we develop and become more mature, certain experiences in life can make it easier for us to identify with more people, communicate with them and therefore increases our emotional intelligence. There is no linear increase with age, however, as EQ skills are developed based on a combination of natural skills and the ability to learn and adapt.

# Conclusion

Emotional intelligence is a valuable set of skills that make communication and interaction with other people much more effective. It fosters a better understanding of how people react, think, and behave and why. The more we aim to understand and empathize with people, the more effective we become in improving our overall interaction with people in general. In conclusion, the following questions are designed to self-examine how well you understand the concept of EQ and how well developed your emotional intelligence is at the present. There are no right or wrong answers, nor is there any scorecard to track how well or poorly you achieve EQ. Every answer is a window into possible improvement and self-reflection:

➢ Are you aware of another person's physical reaction and gestures during a conversation? This may include fidgeting, shifting their body weight, drifting away from the conversation, etc.

➢ When you make a mistake, do you admit that you're wrong and try to reconcile?

➢ Are you able to put aside differences with other people to get along with them and try to work together?

➢ Can you identify the emotion you are experiencing at any given time?

➢ Are you able to let go of anger and move forward from past occurrences?

➢ Before you initiate a conversation, do you observe people's body language and non-verbal cues to determine if it is a good time, and approach accordingly?

 Can you express yourself in a firm, concise manner without becoming angry or personal towards others?

Achieving high EQ skills is an integral part of our development as social beings. Even the most introverted and socially awkward people in society appreciate connecting with other people and finding acceptance with others. It's also normal to want to withdraw at times and avoid human contact, especially when some situations or people become difficult and challenging. When we interact, we want to connect in such a way that we are understood and respected for what we say and how we feel. Validating is a powerful way to bridge the gap between people and groups who don't share the same viewpoints, and often find more ways of conflict than anything else. When we validate and acknowledge the importance of connecting and communicating despite differences in opinion and belief becomes a priority. The more we embrace developing our emotional intelligence, the more we advance as individuals and as a society.